WHITE STAR
PUBLISHERS

CONTENTS

Graphic design
Maria Cucchi

© 2005 White Star S.r.l.
Via Candido Sassone, 22/24
13100 Vercelli, Italy
www.whitestar.it

TRANSLATION:
AMY CHRISTINE EZRIN

ISBN 88-544-0063-7

REPRINTS :
1 2 3 4 5 6   09 08 07 06 05

Printed in China
Color separation Fotomec, Turin

Mexico

PLACES AND HISTORY

Text by Davide Domenici

1 A mask portraying the rain god Chac (or maybe other gods, but always with a long "nose" as a divine attribute) extends out from a corner of the Nunnery Quadrangle in Uxmal.

2-7 The Temple of the Frescoes in Bonampak provides a series of extraordinary wall paintings, which illustrate the bellicose enterprises of the local sovereigns.

3-6 A plethora of influences show in the excited scene of El Agitador, a part of the mural painted by Diego Rivera between 1926 and 1927 in the chapel of the Autonomous University of Chapingo.

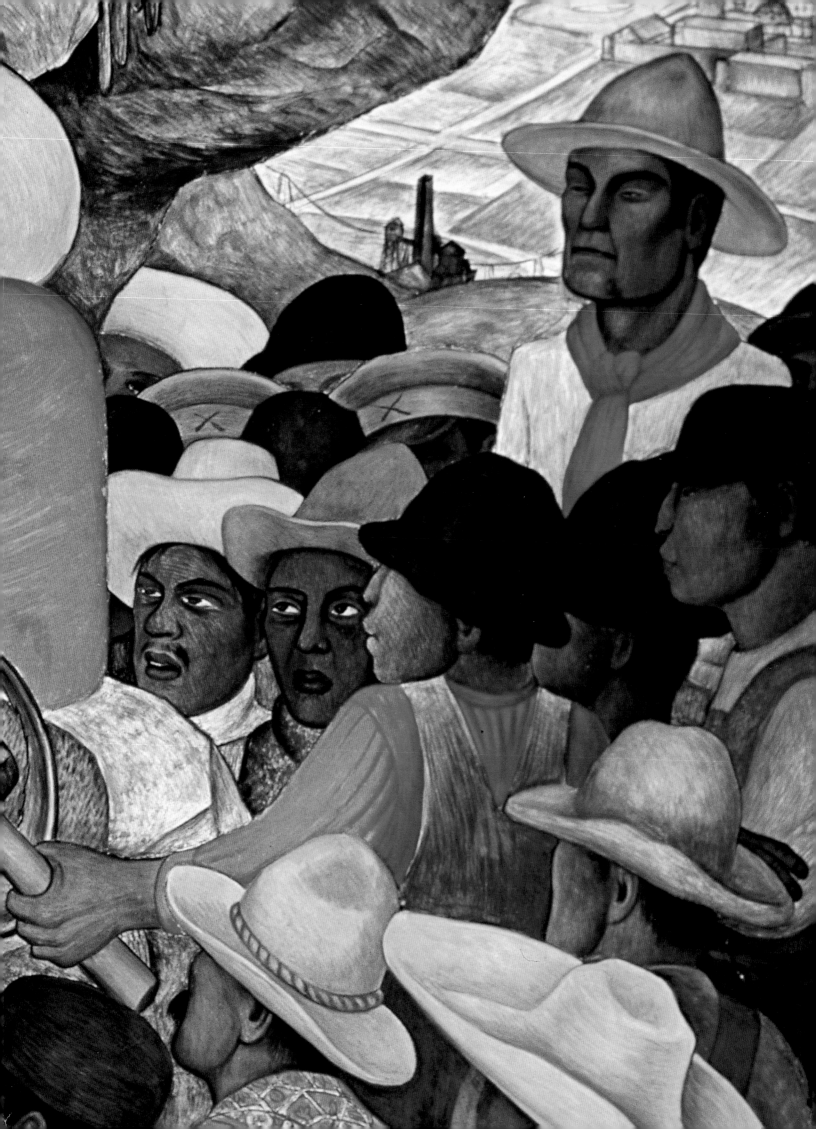

INTRODUCTION

9 top left The Pyramid of Kukulkan, or "El Castillo," rises above the forest surrounding Chichén Itzá in the Yucatán. The building, dated to the 10th century A.D., was consecrated to the serpent god, who is believed to have brought light to the city by means of his superior understanding of science.

9 top right The magnificent Pyramid of the Magician, featuring a unique elliptical base, has dominated the Yucatán site of Uxmal since the 10th century A.D., exhibiting one of the finest examples of the refined "Puuc style."

8 bottom King Pacal of Palenque was buried in the Pyramid of the Inscriptions (detail seen above). The building has yielded the extraordinary funerary furnishings of the sovereign, including what is most likely his portrait in stucco (bottom).

8-9 Rows of lesser pyramids line the Avenue of the Dead, in Teotihuacán, dominated to the east by the imposing Pyramid of the Sun, culminating at 213 feet tall. The structure has been perfectly preserved, with the exception of the actual temple at the very top.

Describing Mexico, its regions, cities and its history is a challenging yet exciting task. Few countries in the world can actually boast an archaeological, environmental, and urban heritage as vast and varied as that of Mexico, formed over the course of nearly 5000 years, covering the pre-Hispanic, colonial, and modern eras.

During the pre-Hispanic period, the more than 750,000 square miles of the present-day Mexican Republic were the setting for the development of civilizations that occupied an outstanding position in the world of their day. In fact, Mesoamerica was, along with the Andean world, one of the two centers of "early civilization" in the New World's two continents, in a class comparable to those of Egypt, Mesopotamia, China, and the Indus Valley in the Old World.

Agriculture, writing, cities, and states are only a few of the cultural phenomena that spontaneously evolved in Mesoamerica; they provide an idea of how much an understanding of Mexico's past, often perceived as exotically interesting but generally simple, is a fundamental chapter in the story of humanity. Civilizations such as the Olmec, Mayan, Zapotec, and Aztec developed diverse and sophisticated artistic traditions from which it is possible to discern the religious concepts, political ideologies, and historical events of the indigenous Mesoamerican world, a world that has not had the privilege to continue its evolution into the present.

Mexico was one of the main theaters of the great tragedy of the Spanish Conquest, one of the most appalling genocides in the history of humanity, which left the indigenous world defeated and mutilated, forced to adapt itself to ideas and lifestyles arrived suddenly from an alien world. From its encounter – and clash – with the Americas, which happens to mark the beginning of the modern era, Europe drew both a new conscience and immense wealth, the foundation stones of the development of capitalism and the socioeconomic processes still in place today. However, Mexico is not a country to cry over spilt milk: the clash of cultures was in some way transformed into a meeting that, despite being born of pain and violence, gave life to a new world, the hybrid world of present-day Mexico, complete with its contradictions and internal divisions.

Pre-Hispanic ruins, colonial churches, and modern glass skyscrapers co-exist in a country whose population is composed

of Indians, people of mixed race, and Caucasians. From this inextricable mixture, it has nonetheless known how to extract the vital life force. The various ethnic components of the Mexican identity, the country's wealth, and the peculiar events of its modern history hinging on the revolution have made Mexico a country unique in Latin America. Like few others, it has cross-examined its cultural identity, with which, despite being largely artificial and intellectually constructed, it has been able to give meaning to its flag.

Today, Mexico finds itself at a key point in its development. To cite a famous definition that the well-known anthropologist Guillermo Bonfil Batalla has provided, it can be said that Mexico as it imagines itself (through post-revolutionary cultural redrafting) has previously tried to "redeem" the Mexico of the past, the native and traditional country, in order to absorb it into the national culture. Thus it has appropriated all the ancient symbols that could be useful in the construction of the *mestizo* nation's image. Mexico of the past continues to surface more and more, thereby initiating a phase of attrition and conflict with the expectations of the imagined Mexico, a phase that is, however, also a phase of great vitality.

However, the entire history of Mexico is made up of convulsive and often violent phases: it is a country that seems to have known how to draw energy from every tragedy, which has known every time how to rise from the ruins of its past with a new face. Perhaps the key words to understanding Mexico are "coexistence" and "diversity." Across the wide variety of climates in the Mexican territory and under its appropriately renowned sky, different traditions, dramatically opposed economic conditions, antiquity and modernity, nationalistic rhetoric, and artistic vitality live side by side.

10 top As a symbol of the "victory" of Christianity over pre-Hispanic religions, the convent of San Antonio de Padua, in Izamal in the Yucatán, was built over the foundations of a pyramid consecrated to Chac.

10 bottom A somber, very long, and brightly painted façade distinguishes the imposing convent of San Antonio de Padua in Izamal. The building has stood since 1549, but it was renovated in the late 1800s.

10-11 Impressive tourist resorts rise high in Cancún, one of the most famous vacation spots in the world. What is now a city with 300,000 inhabitants was built in the 1970s on a small island just off the coast of the state of Quintana Roo, in the Yucatán.

11 top left The cathedral of Mexico City is the main symbol of the conversion of conquered Mexico. The first building to be built in what was previously the sacred enclosure of the Templo Mayor was erected in 1524; the present-day cathedral was completed in 1813.

11 top right A Tzotzli woman sews a garment in front of her shop, in the Mayan village of Zinacantan in Chiapas. In Mexico, spinning, weaving, and dyeing in bright colors boasts centuries of history.

USA

Tijuana · Mexicali
Ensenada

Ciudad Juarez

Isla Angel de la Guardia

Hermosillo

Chihuahua

Baja California

Isla Cedros

Isla Tiburon

Sierra Madre Occidental

El Vizcaíno Promontory

Gulf of California

Torreón

Sierra Madre Oriental

Monterrey

Culiacán

La Paz

Durango

Mazatlán

Cabo San Lucas

Islas Tres Marias

San Luis Potosí

Aguascalientes
León
Querétaro

Pacific Ocean

Guadalajara

Tula
Teotihuacán
Mexico City

Toluca
Cuernavaca
Xochicalco

Sierra Madre del Sur

Acapulco

14-15 Paradise for boaters, the Sea of Cortés stretches in a northwest-southeast direction along the west coast of Mexico. Separating its relatively warm and calm waters from those of the Pacific Ocean, the thin peninsula of Baja California is full of unspoiled places.

16-17 Seeing the "Castillo," the main complex of buildings at the Tulum site, in 1518 must have greatly impressed the Spanish just after landing on the shores of the Yucatán. At that time, in fact, the city appeared as a solid fortress, outfitted with walls and watchtowers.

Gulf of
Mexico

• Tampico

• El Tajín

• Veracruz

Puebla

Coatzacoalcos

• Villahermosa

Monte
Albán

• Milla

Tuxtla
Gutiérrez

Palenque

B e l i z e

Oaxaca

San Cristóbal
de las Casas

Puerto
Escondido

• Merida

Uxmal

Chichén
Itzá

• Cancún

Cobá

Kabah

Tulum

G u a t e m a l a

*T*he bubbling melting-pot of peoples, languages, cities, monuments, foods, types of music, colors, and traditions called Mexico is the result of thousands of years of a history that is both tragic and grand, a history composed of great ancient civilizations, unspeakable massacres, a profound longing for freedom, and ferocious repression. Over the course of centuries, Indians, Africans, Creoles, and *mestizos* have each in their own way contributed to the birth of a country whose history resembles a multicolored cloth woven through with the threads of so many different stories, inseparably brought together by fate. Examining the history of Mexico requires studying the course of multiple and conflicting Mexican histories. The remote origins of the indigenous Mexican population are still largely shrouded by the mists of the past. It is known, however, that since at least 30,000 years ago, the Mexican territory was visited by groups of hunter-gatherers that reached the American continent by way of the Bering Strait. Since then, the environmental variety of the country and the climatic changes that have affected it have given rise to several cultural traditions tied to economic specializations such as hunting large Pleistocene-era animals or gathering wild plants in the vast, arid expanses of the north. Precisely because of this latter activity, the first steps toward the do-

mestication of plant species were taken, which brought about the emergence of the earliest agricultural communities around 2500 B.C. The spread of farming techniques led to the subdivision of the present-day Mexican territory into three large cultural zones: Aridamerica, Oasiamerica, and Mesoamerica. In Aridamerica, an area of vast desert expanses covering northern Mexico and a large part of the southwestern United States, the ancient hunting and

18 For thousands of years, the hunter-gatherers of the American continents used tools made from splintered stone. The two knives pictured here, in flint, were glued to a wooden handle by means of plant resin: such technology continued to be used by groups settled in the northern regions of Mesoamerica and Aridamerica until the end of the 17th century.

18-19 The first colonists came to the American continents by crossing a now-submerged land bridge, located in what is now the present-day Bering Strait and created by the shrinking of sea levels during the last Ice Age. Although the date of the event is still the object of discussion, the migration most likely happened over 30,000 years ago.

gathering system continued until the colonial era. The Indians living in this region organized themselves into small, highly mobile nomadic groups, often dedicated to raiding rival tribes. Their diet was based on the seeds, berries, nuts, and cactus that they could gather. Adaptation to an environment that was in many ways extreme led to an equally extreme lifestyle that greatly amazed the first European observers. They noted two practices in particular: the *maroma* and the "second harvest." The first practice consisted of tying a piece of meat to a leather strap; the meat was swallowed, then extracted from the stomach, and then passed to another family member until it was completely digested. The second referred to individuals picking undigested cactus seeds from their feces and then toasting them in order to eat them again. Aridamerica was overall the world of the warlike nomads that the Aztecs called Chichimechi, or "Dog People." On the other hand, on a kind of "island" in the far north of present-day Mexico, in the northern part of the present-day states of Sonora and Chihuahua, more promising environmental conditions allowed for the development of a farming community in what was a "Mexican limb" of Oasiamerica. This was the larger cultural area where the Hohokam, Mogollon, Anasazi, and Pueblo peoples of the southwestern United States flourished.

19

20 *The Old God of Fire, known during the era of the Aztecs as Huehueteotl (Old God), was one of the first divinities to be worshiped in Central Mexico. His cult was also probably related to the intense volcanic activity of the region.*

21 *The Lord of Las Limas (Veracruz) is one of the most beautiful stone sculptures produced by the Olmec civilization, the first of the great Mesoamerican civilizations to develop in the southern part of the coast of the Gulf of Mexico between 1200 and 400 B.C.*

South of the Tropic of Cancer extended Mesoamerica, the zone that saw the development of great cultures such as the Mayan, Aztec (Nahuan), and Zapotec. The border between Mesoamerica and Aridamerica was actually formed by a mobile and permeable line. At the time of the Conquest, it coincided approximately with the 25°N parallel, but it is known that during previous centuries some groups of farmers had journeyed even farther north, colonizing lands only to abandon them again well before the arrival of the Europeans.

The beginning of Mesoamerican farming activity customarily marks the start of the Lower Pre-Classical period (2500-1200 B.C.). This epoch was characterized by the spread of farming community villages upon which the foundations of the common Mesoamerican culture were built: agriculture based on corn, beans, hot peppers, and squashes; a society organized by patrilineal descent; the tripartite conception of the cosmos; a 260-day ritual calendar; etc.

A progressive increase in hierarchization and social complexity during the Middle Pre-Classical period (1200-400 B.C.) led to the emergence of stratified political entities in areas such as the Mexican Basin, the Oaxaca Valley, the Gulf Coast, the Pacific Coast of Chiapas and in the Mayan lands of Chiapas, Guatemala, Belize, and Honduras. Among these regions, that of the Gulf Coast, populated by groups speaking Mixe-zoque languages, soon took on a preeminent role

in as much as it was the center of the Olmec civilization's development. Towns such as San Lorenzo and La Venta became veritable capitals of the Olmec aristocracy, in which a tradition of monumental sculpture developed that remains one of the high points of Mesoamerican art. Here, the Olmec kings were portrayed with colossal heads and seated on great basalt thrones, placed in the vicinity of pyramids and other packed-earth structures. The Olmec aristocracy composed

the central hub of a vast pan-Mesoamerican commercial network through which flowed luxury goods (jade, ceramics, feathers, skins, etc.) that were the status symbols sought by emerging ruling classes to emphasize and justify the sacred nature of their authority. In this sense, Olmec artistic style became a sort of *lingua franca* of Mesoamerican rulers, an expression of cosmological and political concepts that culturally united the entire region.

With the disappearance of the unifying influence of the Olmec political entity, over the course of the late Pre-Classical period (400 B.C.- A.D. 300), Mesoamerica underwent an intense period of regional differentiation during which the great ethno-cultural groups of the subsequent Classical period took shape. Monte Albán became the capital of the Zapotec state of Oaxaca. Teotihuacán grew to dominate the entire Mexican Basin, transforming itself into the most important city on the American continents. In the Mayan world, the colonization of the lowlands covered by tropical forest brought about the foundation of cities like Mirador, Uaxactún, Tikal, Calakmul, and Copán. Along the Gulf Coast and in northern Chiapas, settlements such as Tres Zapotes, Cerro de Las Mesas, and Chiapa de Corzo inherited the remaining Olmec authority, becoming the capitals of several Mixe-zoque kingdoms.

Development processes that emerged during the late Pre-Classical were completed during the subsequent Old Classical period (A.D. 300-600), one of the most splendid eras in Mesoamerican history. Teotihuacán, since transformed into a gigantic multiethnic metropolis with over 200,000 inhabitants (the sixth largest city in the world in A.D. 600), became the "sacred city" *par excellence* of Mesoameri-

23 left Characteristic traits identify this terracotta piece found in a tomb in the state of Oaxaca as the "Old God." Sculptures of this kind, mistakenly known as "urns," are an example of the artistic sophistication of the Zapotecs, an ethnic group that populated the area of Oaxaca for thousands of years.

23 right This splendid terracotta jaguar, from whose neck hangs a textile ornament, comes from the city of Monte Albán, which since 500 B.C. had been the capital of the powerful Zapotec state of Oaxaca.

ca. Its rulers conducted important diplomatic and commercial relations with the Zapotecs of Monte Albán and with the sovereigns of the royal Mayan dynasties. A vast commercial network dominated by Teotihuacán – which probably held a sort of monopoly over the obsidian trade – linked all of Mesoamerica, from the northerly expanding area of the Chalchihuites culture (Zacatecas and Durango) to the regions of Central America (Honduras, El Salvador, etc.).

Relations were particularly intense between Teotihuacán and the Mayan cities of Tikal and Copán, whose kings boasted political-diplomatic connections with the central Mexican metropolis. Tikal, after having militarily defeated the nearby Uaxactún, became the most important Mayan city in the lowlands, the seat of one of the most magnificent and long-lasting royal dynasties in all of Mesoamerica, in constant conflict with the rulers of Caracol and Calakmul. The hieroglyphic writing system and the complex Mesoamerican calendar, drafted during the previous period, were brought to their highest levels of complexity in the Mayan world, becoming fundamental elements of religious-propagandistic inscriptions. Sculptures, bas-reliefs, and frescoes multiplied in number, adorning palaces and temples in the monumental cities of the gorgeous "jungle capitals."

26 top Four Serpents of Fire are portrayed on this wooden disc covered by a turquoise mosaic that comes from Chichén Itzá (Yucatán). The relic attests to the adoption of stylistic features typical of Central Mexico by the Post-classic Mayan world.

26 bottom Portraits of the god Quetzalcoatl occupy two pages of a pre-Hispanic codex, constituted of a single strip of paper made from vegetable fiber and folded like an accordion.

27 Among the most important ritual activities of high Mayan nobility was self-sacrifice. On this lintel from Yaxchilan, a queen can be seen as she passes a thorny rope through her perforated tongue, under the gaze of her husband. From the blood collected in a bowl below, the Serpent of Visions supposedly surfaced, from whose fangs emerged the deceased ancestors evoked by the ritual.

At the beginning of the Late Classical period (A.D. 600-900), the fall of Teotihuacán, burned and partially abandoned around A.D. 650, paved the way for upheavals of enormous proportions in Mesoamerican political stability. Upon the collapse of Teotihuacán, the Mayan, Zapotec, and Mixe-zoque worlds experienced their most splendid periods. In central Mexico, where the earliest penetration of groups of northern origin took place, new political entities like Xochicalco, Cacaxtla, Teotenango, and Tula took advantage of the power void, just as El Tajín did along the Gulf Coast.

Around A.D. 900, however, almost all the great capitals of the past had fallen into abandonment, overwhelmed by the collapse of the entire political-cultural system of classical Mesoamerica that began with the fall of Teotihuacán. The power of Monte Albán was largely eclipsed in the area of Oaxaca by new Zapotec kingdoms and the incipient expansion of hostile Mixtec rulers. The Mayan cities of the southern lowlands were completely abandoned whereas, in the Yucatán Peninsula where the transition was less traumatic, the new many-columned Mayan styles of Chenes, Río Bec, and Puuc gave rise to the growth of new cities such as Kabah, Sayil, Uxmal, and Chichén Itzá. During this same period, those peoples who were previously forced to colonize the northern territories of Guanajuato, San Luis Potosí, Querétaro, Zacatecas, and Durango began to move into the south again. The return of these groups was accompanied by the arrival of tribes of nomadic hunters in Mesoamerica, where they underwent a process of acculturation and into which they imported cultural elements from the north.

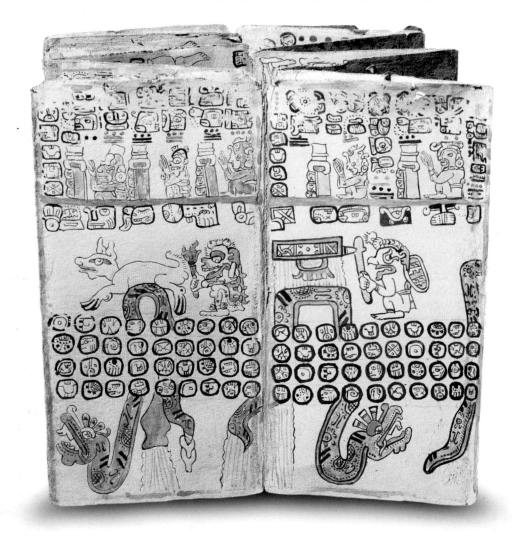

The new sociopolitical balance that settled in the wake of the Classical period took its final form during the Old Post-Classical period (A.D. 900-1200). During this period, the Toltecs of Tula, who owed the majority of their culture to northern traditions, managed to found a vast expansionist empire, which came to dominate a large part of central Mexico and which was based on concepts like holy war and the cult of the Feathered Serpent. The Toltec artistic and political "language" spread throughout all of Mesoamerica in conjunction with a proliferation of multiethnic political entities, often ruled by groups of nobles and no longer by single sovereigns. The different ethnic-cultural traditions of the Classical period started to hybridize, thus giving birth to more homogenous, "international," and widespread artistic forms, as "Mexican" elements (i.e., from central Mexico) began to penetrate strongly into the Mayan realm. There Chichén Itzá had become the capital of a powerful military Mayan state culturally tied to the Toltec world.

28 left The eclectic artistic style of the Epiclassic period (A.D. 650-900) is well evidenced by this wall mural from Cacaxtla (Tlaxcala) portraying a supernatural being, possibly a patron of merchants.

28 right The Toltec art from Tula, represented by this small "Atlas" that may have supported a throne, initiated an "international" style widespread throughout Mesoamerica during the Old Post-Classic period (A.D. 900-1250).

29 top The groups that, starting in the Old Post-Classic period, began to migrate south from the northern lands toward Central Mexico recorded their origins in historical-mythological narratives written in pictographic documents. The colonial-era Tlotzin Map illustrates, for example, the origins of the reigning dynasty of the Nahua city of Texcoco.

y xinacmoztoc onpatla cat
y njotlil xochicin

29 bottom Among the elements of Toltec origin present in the Mayan city of Chichén Itzá (Yucatán), there are the statues known as chac mool. Offerings and the hearts of sacrificed prisoners were placed on the plate in the divinity's lap.

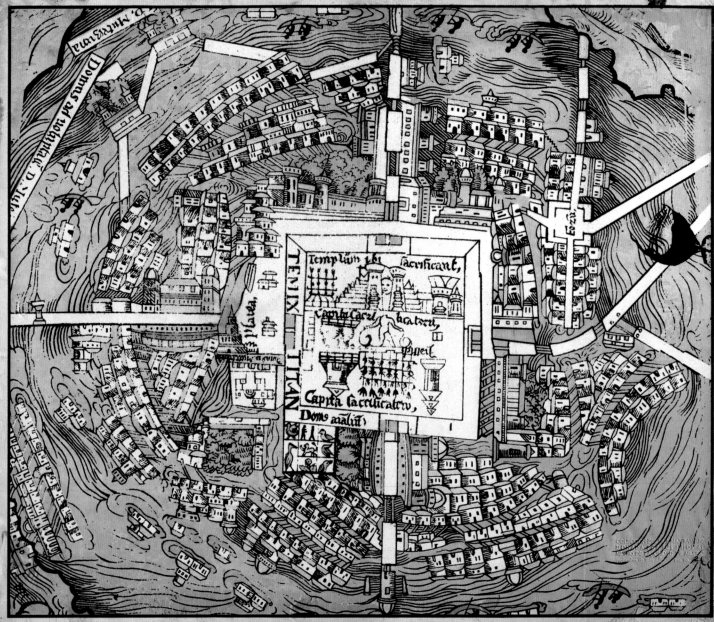

Parte central del Mapa de Cortés, aumentado y a colores para distinguir
la arquitectura de los principales edificios.

30 top left The Aztecs, or Mexicas, told tales of having begun their initial migration from a place called Aztlan, illustrated here on a page in the Boturini Codex. Led by their god Huitzilopochtli, they supposedly came down as far as Central Mexico where they founded their capital Tenochtitlán.

30 top right An Aztec noble bears a fan of feathers in this illustration taken from the Historia de las Indias, written in the 16th century by the Dominican father Diego Duran. An ardent ethnographer, the religious figure produced a work of great importance in reconstructing the customs and lifestyles of pre-Hispanic Mexico.

Around A.D. 1250, new political upsets hit all of Mesoamerica; both Tula and Chichén Itzá were abandoned and, in the Late Post-Classical period (A.D. 1200-1521), their role was assumed by a series of lesser cities, often in competition with each other. The city of Mayapán became the main center of power among the Mayas of the Yucatán, the expansion of Mixtec kingdoms reached the state of Oaxaca, while in central Mexico a constellation of Nahua cities (populated by speakers of Uto-Aztec languages) established an instable political structure, soon overthrown by the arrival of a new Nahua group of northern origin: the Aztecs, or Mexicas.

According to legend, the Mexicas reached the Mexican Basin at the end of a long migratory journey initiated in Aztlan, a mythical place in northern or western Mexico. Once arrived in the Mexican Basin, in 1325 the Mexicas founded Mexico-Tenochtitlán, their new capital built on a small island in the Texcoco Lake. Within just over a century, thanks to remarkable military ability and an alliance with the cities of Texcoco and Tlacopan, Tenochtitlán had already become one of the most important cities in the Mexican Basin.

Between 1469 and 1519, this triple alliance dominated by the Mexicas of Tenochtitlán constructed the vastest expansionist empire that Mexico had ever known. The mystical warrior became the cornerstone of imperial ideology and the impetus for a succession of military campaigns that extended Mexica power over all of central Mexico, along the Gulf Coast, and over part of the Pacific Coast of Chiapas. Very few unconquered areas remained within the imperial borders, while to the south the Mixtecs, Mixe-zoques, and myriad small, independent Mayan kingdoms prospered thanks to intense military and commercial activity.

30 bottom This 17th-century engraving reproduces the map of Tenochtitlán attributed to the conquistador Hernán Cortés, who attached the original to the second letter he sent from Mexico to the king of Spain, Charles V.

31 According to legend, Tenochtitlán stood on the spot indicated by the apparition of an eagle on a prickly-pear bush, a scene depicted on the first page of the Mendoza Codex, seen in the illustration.

33 top left Xochipilli, god of plants and flowers, is portrayed in this statue, probably in a state of ecstasy induced by the ingestion of hallucinogenic plants.

33 bottom right This famous find called "Sun Stone," now held in the Mexico City Museum of Anthropology, is considered one of the emblems of Aztec civilization.

32 One of the cornerstones of imperial Aztec ideology was holy war, waged by a powerful army in which the ranks of the Eagle Warriors and the Jaguar Warriors were foremost. This portrayal of an Eagle Warrior was found in the area of the Templo Mayor, in Tenochtitlan.

34 top The god Tezcatlipoca (Smoking Mirror), one of the main Aztec divinities, was associated with magic and soothsaying. He is seen here portrayed in this mask composed of a human skull covered by a mosaic of turquoise, obsidian, oyster shells, and pyrite.

In particular, the Mixtec world experienced a period of great prosperity following the end of the Classical period. The Mixtec rulers were at the top of a collection of small war-like kingdoms, whose adventures were often the subject of a series of pre-Columbian books, or codices, of extraordinary beauty. The opulence of the Mixtec kings and nobles is well reflected in archaeological finds: splendid gold pieces and handcrafted objects covered with turquoise mosaics attest to the prevalence of an artistic style that spread throughout much of Mesoamerica, profoundly influencing even the art of the Aztecs. At the same time as the Aztec Empire grew steadily, beyond its northwestern border a new, large realm, the Tarasco kingdom, appeared poised to become the main adversary of the Aztec armies just as new catastrophic events interrupted the independent evolution of the indigenous world.

34-35 One of the main artistic techniques used during the Aztec era was turquoise mosaic: seen here, a splendid example is represented by a two-headed serpent portraying Xiuhcoatl (Fire Serpent or Turquoise Serpent), an important Aztec mythological figure.

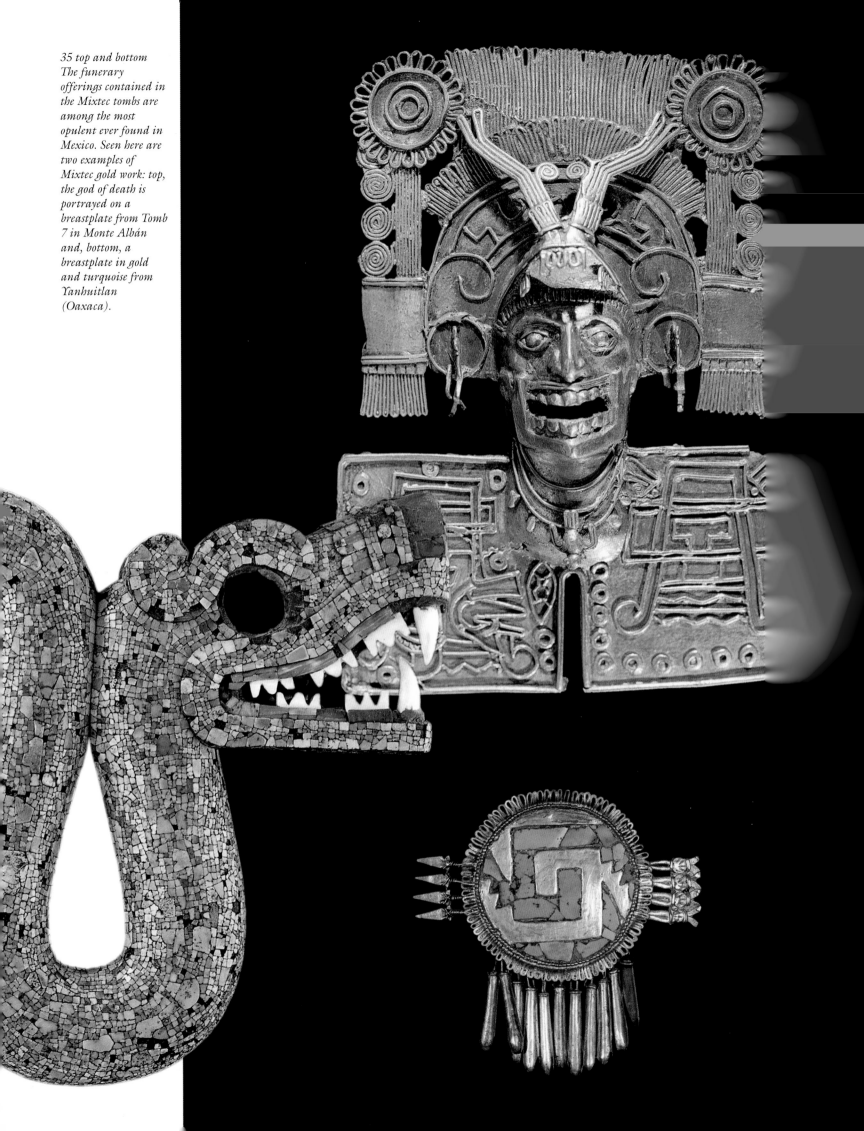

35 top and bottom
The funerary
offerings contained in
the Mixtec tombs are
among the most
opulent ever found in
Mexico. Seen here are
two examples of
Mixtec gold work: top,
the god of death is
portrayed on a
breastplate from Tomb
7 in Monte Albán
and, bottom, a
breastplate in gold
and turquoise from
Yanhuitlan
(Oaxaca).

36 left In 1519, on one of the streets leading to Tenochtitlán, Hernán Cortés and the Aztec King Motecuhzoma Xocoyotzin met for the first time and exchanged gifts. The scene is depicted in a painting on copper dating back to the end of the 18th century or the beginning of the 19th.

36 right After being welcomed deferentially by Motecuhzoma (who may have believed him to be a god) and lodged in one of the royal palaces of the capital, Cortés ordered that the emperor be incarcerated, as illustrated in a painting belonging to the same series as the one seen on the left.

In 1519, while Motecuhzoma Xocoyotzin (Montezuma) reigned over Tenochtitlán, Spanish ships reached the coast of Mexico. They belonged to the expedition of Hernán Cortés, the captain who, with an army of only a few hundred men, was able to bring the Aztec Empire to its knees within two years. Cortés' true weapons were his military and technological superiority based on firearms and horses, his ability to manipulate the internal rivalries of the indigenous world in order to quickly gain thousands of local allies, and his incomparable political unscrupulousness.

Added to this the cargo of diseases that the Spanish unwittingly brought to the New World, a cargo that revealed itself to be the deadliest weapon of conquest known in history. The numbers are uncertain and debatable, but it is general-ly believed that the more than 20,000,000 individuals populating Mesoamerica in 1519 were reduced to only one million within a century. This terrible genocide and the associated processes of acculturation and conversion brought about the rapid dissolution of the native social and cultural fabric, since then forced to survive in almost clandestine conditions in safe regions or in syncretistic and culturally mixed forms.

After the Conquest's early "heroic" period (obviously from the victor's point of view), the settling of the colonial administrative situation reinforced the position of the Spanish crown to the detriment of that of many *hidalgos* and ship captains. These men had for a time had claimed personal control over lands in New Spain, which were then placed under the authority of a viceroy.

The years of the Colony (1521-1821) were years of exploitation and "spiritual conquest" of the native populations, which seemed to quickly accept, at least from the outside, the new religion, abandoning or reducing their ancient beliefs to "underground" forms. This process substantially contributed to the loss in large part of traditional practices, even though it was actually some of the missionaries who deserve the credit for recording beliefs, habits, and native dress in works that today constitute the main sources for studying the indigenous past. Among those chroniclers, the Franciscan Bernardino de Sahagun stands out, the true founder of Latin-American anthropology.

However, the years of the Colony were above all years of devastating economic exploitation of the Mexican lands.

37 left Motecuhzoma Xocoyotzin, portrayed here in an oil painting belonging to the Medici collection and today held in Palazzo Pitti, was unable to react to the surprise of the Spanish arrival. The sovereign was killed over the course of a revolt by the natives during the occupation of Tenochtitlán.

37 top right The severe and narrow face of Hernán Cortés, the shrewd and merciless conqueror of Mexico, is recognizable in this 16th-century portrait. Despite the success of his venture, the conquistador *struggled to reap the benefits he hoped for: once nominated Earl of the Oaxaca Valley, he was soon excluded from the exploitation of the new Spanish colony's enormous wealth.*

Español con India,
Mestizo.

Mestizo con Española
Castizo.

Castizo con Española
Español.

Español con Mora
Mulato.

5

6

7

Mulato con Española,
Morisco.

Morisco con Española
Chino.

Chino con India,
Salta atras.

Salta atras con Mulata,
Lobo.

9

10

11

12

Lobo con China
Gibaro.

Gibaro con Mulata
Albarazado

Albarazado con Negra
Canbujo.

Canbujo con India,
Sanbaigo.

13

14

15

16

Sanbaigo con Loba
Calpamulato.

Calpamulato con Canbuja
Tente en el Aire.

Tente en el Aire, con Mulata
Noteentiendo.

Noteentiendo con India
Tornaatras.

38 The meeting of white men, natives, and slaves soon set off a radical phenomenon of racial integration. Attempts to "control" this process lead to the spread of the pinturas de castas, in which the offspring of all the possible interracial unions were meticulously classified.

A Chiametlan
B Guadalajara
C Chiapa
D Gueveltan
E Vera Pax
F Tabasco
G Costa Rica
H Veragua

39 top New Spain, illustrated here in a 17th-century map, was soon subjected to the authority of a Viceroy who governed in the name of the Spanish crown, managing above all the massive flow of precious metals coming from deposits discovered in northern Mexico.

In the north, exploitation of the country's mines fueled the colonization of the lands of Aridamerica until the middle of the 17th century. In southern regions, on the other hand, the model of the farming *hacienda* became the main productive unit, around which great swathes of land were gathered under the direct control of the *hacendado*. The *hacienda* was also the fundamental cell of the system of the *encomienda,* on the basis of which the crown gave the *encomendero* the right to use a territory and its population, thus demanding work and tributes in exchange for a "commitment" to conversion and the "civilization" of the natives. Though this new economic balance usurped the lands of the native communities and in effect often reduced the natives to slavery, the Spanish political policy of the *congregaciónes* (the concentration of scattered rural communities scattered into centralized settlements for easier control) caused the final breakdown of the indigenous territorial organization.

The political and cultural situation in the Spanish colonies across the ocean began to change around the middle of the 18th century, when the ideas of the Enlightenment started to spread to the American continents. New Spain had by now expanded militarily to include Texas, California, New Mexico, and Arizona, thus covering over 1,500,000 square miles and containing 6,000,000 inhabitants. Of the latter, 60 percent were natives, 20 percent *mestizo,* 4 percent Spanish, and 16 percent Creole. It was the Creoles, those individuals of Spanish blood but born on American soil, to usher in the new cultural climate along with demands for progressive independence from the Spanish mother country. The 18th century was, in fact, a century of constant economic growth in mining, agriculture, and manufacturing, but only the Spanish component of the Mexican population enjoyed the profits. Alexander von Humboldt, the great German geographer-explorer who traveled to Mexico in 1803, wrote, "Mexico is the country of inequality; a tremendous inequality exists in the distribution of wealth and culture."

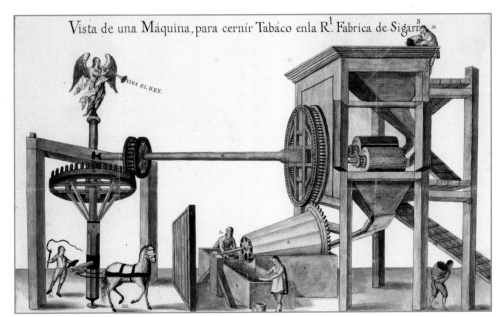

39 bottom Over the course of the 18th century, New Spain experienced a period of intense manufacturing expansion encouraged by the dominant Spanish social class. In a print from that period, a machine for processing tobacco is seen, one of the plants whose use was introduced into Europe after the discovery of the Americas.

The Creoles thus became the promoters of independence movements and anti-Spanish conspiracies, to the extent that from 1810, under the guidance of priests Miguel Hidalgo and José Maria Morelos, they assumed the tones of a full-out war of independence. On September 28, 1821, the first independent Mexican government was installed in Mexico City under the leadership of Colonel Agustín Iturbide, the "Father of the Homeland." He was actually an exponent of the wealthy classes, who saw it as highly possible to obtain independence without, however, having to realize social reforms. In May 1822, Iturbide was nominated emperor under the name of

Agustín I, a title that he was, however, forced to give up the next year when the Republic was restored.

The early decades in independent Mexico saw a succession of clashes between the *caudillos*, presidential appointees who were immediately unseated by military uprisings, and constitutions enacted only to be quickly annulled. Between 1821 and 1850, there were 50 governments, eleven of which presided over by Antonio Lopez de Santa Anna. The economy experienced a long period of crisis, and between 1845 and 1848, United States troops conquered California, Nevada, New Mexico, and Utah even getting so far as to raise the United States flag over the National Palace of Mexico City. In 1848, the War of the Castes, the most significant Mayan rebellion yet, flared up, putting the Yucatán to fire and sword for several years. Meanwhile, groups of Apache, Mayo, and Yaqui Indians led raids on the northern regions of the country. The 1850s were marked by rough conflict, in many cases military, between the conservative and liberal parties. In fact, a leader from the latter party, the Zapotec Indian Benito Juárez, having assumed the presidency, enacted the Laws of the Reformation (1859), establishing the nationalization of church possessions, civil marriage, the closure of convents, the secularization of cemeteries, and the suppression of many religious holidays. These measures unleashed the fierce reaction of powerful European countries. In 1862, Napoleon III's French troops invaded Mexico, and Maximilian von Habsburg, the archduke of Austria, was nominated Emperor of Mexico. However, his reign was brief: the liberal armies defeated the French in 1867 and Maximilian was executed by firing squad. With the fall of Maximilian, the Republic was restored under the leadership of none other than Benito Juárez, the national hero who held the presidency until his death in 1872, upon which he was replaced by Sebastián Lerdo de Tejada.

40 top United States troops entered Mexico City on September 14, 1847 under the command of General Winfield Scott, veteran of the Indian Wars and later a distinguished official of the American Civil War. In the war with the United States (1846-1848), Mexico lost nearly half of its national territory.

40 bottom Independence from Spain, despite being handled largely by the country's elite Creole class, constituted a fundamental step in the formation of a new Mexican national identity. Protagonists of the Independence, among them Miguel Hidalgo, recognizable by his white hair, are portrayed in the middle of this fresco by Diego Rivera, which adorns a wall in the National Palace of Mexico City.

40-41 The French invasion of Mexico culminated in the battle of Puebla, on March 29, 1863. In the painting by Jean Adolphe Beauce, the siege of Fort San Xavier de Puebla by the French army under the command of General Bazaine is depicted.

1877 was a key year in the modern history of Mexico: Porfirio Díaz, a hero of the war against the French and a conservative political adversary of Juárez, was elected president of the Republic, thus initiating the 34 years of the *porfiriato*. The mottoes "zero percent politics, 100 percent administration" and "order and progress" forcefully summarized the *porfiriato*'s strategy, and from the economic and infrastructural development viewpoint, it was characterized by swift modernization in some sectors of the country, in an attempt to emulate European states like Britain, France, and Italy. At the same time, however, it notably widened the gap between rich and poor, as compliance with democratic ideals came to be reduced in such a way that Porfirio Díaz's reign (re-elected president seven times in succession) essentially evolved into a dictatorship.

The rebellion against the Díaz dictatorship exploded a few months after his last reelection, when in November 1910 Francisco I. Madero led, to cries of "real suffrage, no reelection," the armed uprising that initiated the Mexican Revolution and that put him in the presidential office in November 1911. Nonetheless, revolutionary movements continued for a good ten years, with the uprising of several *caudillos* such as Pascual Orozco, Francisco Villa, Emiliano Zapata, Alvaro Obregón, and Venustiano Carranza, bearers of various social demands who often found themselves in conflict with each other and opposed to Victoriano Huerta's counterrevolutionary forces. In the end, in 1920, Alvaro Obregón, a successful soldier and a representative of the middle class, assumed the presidential position, initiating the reconstruction of the nation.

42-43 The Mexican Revolution was one of the most significant political events of the 20th century, and a large part of the development of a national identity over the last century was based on it, often using tools of a nationalistic-rhetorical nature. In the photograph, taken in 1911, a group of revolutionary women and girls pose for the photographer.

43 top left Unlike other revolutionary caudillos, Emiliano Zapata never gave in to the lure of power and is still remembered today as the "purest" symbol of the revolutionary spirit.

43 top right The Mexican regions where the revolutionary uprising was the greatest at first were those in the north. In the period photo, the entrance of revolutionary troops into the city of Sinaloa in November 1913 can be seen.

43 center Pancho Villa was without doubt, next to Zapata, the most famous of the caudillos of the revolution.

43 bottom The Zapatista rebels march on Xochimilco on August 15, 1914 to the call of "tierra y libertad."

45 top center
President Portas Gil
listens to the reading
of a proclamation
regarding the
distribution of lands
to farmers in the
state of Hidalgo.

45 bottom center
Cuauhtémoc
Cárdenas, son of
Lazaro Cárdenas,
was the founder
of the first Mexican
opposition party, born
of an internal break-
up of the Institutional
Revolutionary Party.
Defeated two times in
presidential elections,

in 1997 he was elected
mayor of Mexico City,
thus becoming the first
politician not
belonging to the
IRP to assume
an important
institutional position.

45 bottom Although
Mexico went through
a period of notable
economic and social
development in the
post-revolutionary
era, its political life
was completely
dominated by one
party called the
Institutional
Revolutionary Party.

The early post-revolutionary period was an era of great social progress and cultural fervor, largely fomented by the education minister José Vasconcelos. Besides an intensive reorganization of the school system, he commissioned works of significant social and educational content from the muralist Diego Rivera, José Clemente Orozco, and David Alfaro Siqueiros, giving rise to one of Mexico's livelier cultural eras. Lasting until after the First World War, the period even boasted the participation of artists like Frida Kahlo and Rufino Tamayo.

Though the social and cultural condition of Mexico progressively improved, its political situation continued to be far from a true democracy. In 1928, the official government party was founded (today the Institutional Revolutionary Party, or IRP): since then, the history of Mexican politics and that of the IRP have coincided for the entire 20th century, with each new president basically nominated by the last.

Among the more important events in modern Mexican history, the presidency of Lazaro Cárdenas (1934-1940), who enacted farming reform and nationalized the oil reserves, was particularly outstanding. After the participation, albeit limited, of Mexico in the Second World War, the country proceeded on its path of economic development, largely petroleum-based, which coincided with an enormous demographic boom and an ever-increasing restriction of constitutional rights. The anti-government student demonstrations organized during the Olympic Games of 1968 were violently repressed by the police, featuring the sadly well-known massacre of Tlatelolco Square.

Over the course of the 1970s and 80s, the country experienced a profound crisis linked to the collapse of oil prices, causing fierce social tensions – aggravated by events like the devastating earthquake that hit the capital in 1985 – and rising criticism of the government party. In 1988, the official candidate Salinas de Gortari defeated the opposition candidate Cuauhtémoc Cárdenas, son of the ex-president, in presidential elections riddled with corruption suspicions.

44 Diego Rivera was
the muralist painter to
whom was entrusted
the most important
commission of post-
revolutionary Mexico.
Among his more
famous subjects, besides
episodes from Mexican
history, there are the
"flower vendors" like
the one in the
illustration, proper
icons of Mexican art.

45 top General
Lazaro Cárdenas,
veteran of the
revolution, was the
most important
Mexican president of
the 20th century,
responsible for the
nationalization of the
oil industry that
brought Mexico to
within a step away
from its conflict with
the United States.

46 left The electoral victory of Vicente Fox, ex-president of Coca-Cola in Mexico and Latin America, marked the end of the IRP's domination of Mexican politics. A supporter of the liberalistic upper class, under his presidency Mexico has launched a neo-free-trade policy that has exacerbated the social conflicts that already plague the country.

46 right A new revolutionary icon, Sub-commander Marcos became the emblem of the neo-Zapatista rebellion that broke out on January 1, 1994 in the state of Chiapas. The revolt shattered the neo-free-trade dreams of the country, bringing to the light the existence of unresolved ancient conflicts "deep in the heart" of Mexico.

46-47 A group of natives guards the borders of their community. The Zapatista revolt and the counter-attacks of the regular army brought about the outbreak of conflicts between communities among the indigenous peoples of Chiapas belonging mainly to the Tzotzil, Tzeltal, and Tojolabal Mayan ethnic groups.

President Salinas' highly neo-liberalist policies were revealed in a rush of privatizations and his signing of the free-trade agreement with the United States and Canada (NAFTA), which took effect on January 1, 1994. That same day, however, Mexico experienced the greatest political upset of its recent history: on the night of New Year's Day, the native Mayans of the Zapatista National Liberation Army, led by *subcomandante* Marcos, occupied San Cristóbal de Las Casas and three other towns in Chiapas, setting off a rebellion still underway today. Better living conditions, medical services, educational structures, and the restitution of farmlands to the native population feature among the objectives declared by the Zapatistas, thus drawing on the unforgotten legacy of Emiliano Zapata.

In 2000, the IRP was defeated for the first time in the presidential elections by the opposition right-wing candidate. The present-day president of the Republic, Vicente Fox, ex-president of the Coca-Cola Company for Mexico and Latin America, is also the advocate of neo-liberalist policies centered on trade relations with the United States.

Today, Mexico is divided between its high economic goals and the resolution of internal conflicts that are the awkward legacy of its colonial history. However, the energy needed to break out of this impasse will certainly come from the Mexico that is heir to the great libertarian aspirations of the past, the Mexico of the exiled, the Mexico of the artists, the Mexico that has for centuries called out loud for *tierra y libertad*.

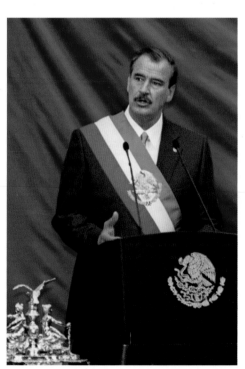

47 bottom left The Zapatista march that got as far as the capital in March 2001 under the leadership of Sub-commander Marcos ended in an epic event: for the first time, an Indian woman, Commander Esther, spoke to the Federal Congress, specifying the demands of the poorest and most discriminated-against part of the country.

47 bottom right Although the Zapatista revolt was characterized by military-type episodes, the true strategic weapon of the Zapatista Army of National Liberation was the clever use of means of communication, which allowed them to attract international attention and hinder military repression.

THE COUNTRY OF EXTREMES

48 The landscape of vast areas of Mexico, from the coastline to the elevated hinterlands, is the realm of a variety of species of cacti and succulent plants. Outstanding among them are agaves, from which fiber is produced for weaving and, in the case of the blue agave, the well-known liquor tequila.

48-49 Giant waves swell along the west coast of Baja California near the promontory of Cabo San Lucas.

Shaped like a funnel at the bottom of North America, the Mexican Republic stretches over an area of over 750,000 square miles, today subdivided into 31 states and one federal district. From a natural environment point of view, the Mexican territory is in many ways extreme: enormous deserts, imposing mountain chains, snowbound volcanoes, dense tropical forests, and gorgeous beaches form a naturalistic mosaic of incredible variety. Today, in a territory that covers not even 2 percent of the earth's surface live 10 percent of the plants, mammals, reptiles, and birds on the face of the planet.

From a physiographic point of view, the outstanding element in Mexican geography is the double "spine" formed by the Sierra Madre Occidental and the Sierra Madre Oriental.

The two mountain chains run north to south, joining at the Central Plateau and continuing on until they become the single mountain chain of the Sierra Madre del Sur, descending toward Guatemala and the other countries of Central America.

The various configurations of the Sierra Madre thus form a "wishbone" of cold highlands rising out of the hot and humid tropical lowlands, which "embraces" the vast expanses of arid deserts to the far north.

Below the Tijuana-Mexicali section of the more than 1,800 miles of border that Mexico shares with the United States extends the Baja California peninsula, "the amputated arm of Mexico," still today one of the Republic's most pristine and least populated regions, full of parks and nature reserves. The slopes of the tall mountain chains on the peninsula overlook two gorgeous coastlines, that of the Pacific and that of the Sea of Cortés, as well as some of the most spectacular marine environments in Mexico. Moving down along the Carretera Transpeninsular as far as the central desert, one enters a lunar landscape made of granite boulders and cactus.

The endemic plants *cirio* (*Idria columnaris*) and the elephant tree (*Pachycormus discolor*) and animals such as deer, rabbits, and bighorn goats are typical of this region, nearly 10,000 square miles of which are protected within the El Vizcáino Biosphere Reserve, the largest in Latin America.

The zone overlooks a stretch of sea constituting an important reproduction site for whales, visible for example in the area of Isla Cedros or in the vicinity of Laguna San Ignacio, also full of cormorants and fish hawks. Inland from San Ignacio, some of the most beautiful rock paintings to be found in North America, those of the Sierra de San Francisco, can be admired.

Today, in the region of Los Cabos, the southernmost part of Baja California, unfortunately spoiled in large part by heavy tourism, some of the finest beaches on the peninsula and, above all, spectacular mountain landscapes grooved by canyons in the Sierra de la Laguna Biosphere Reserve can be explored.

50-51 Isla Espíritu Santo emerges from the deep blue of the Sea of Cortés, almost at the southernmost tip of Baja California. These waters are highly important for the conservation of hundreds of animal species, including 30 marine mammals, 500 fish species, and nearly 5,000 types of small invertebrates, in addition to 600 types of macro-algae.

51 top left Captivating chromatic contrasts brighten up the harsh landscape of the Sierra de San Lazaro, near Cabo San Lucas, the southern point of Baja California.

51 top right Numerous species of birds, both sedentary and migratory, populate the skies and cliffs of Baja California. In the photo, flocks of sea gulls crowd a beach in the south of the peninsula.

50 top The Sea of Cortés is populated by myriads of marine creatures, including several shark species. In the image, a dense group of hammerhead sharks (Sphyrna lewini) explores the medium-deep waters in search of prey.

50 center A common seasonal visitor of the Baja California coast is the large elephant seal (Mirounga angustirostris), which migrates every year from Alaska to the Mexican coastline, where it comes to reproduce.

50 bottom Its head crusted with barnacles, an adult gray whale surfaces off the coast of Baja California. The lagoons of El Vizcáino, natural sanctuaries famous for the cetaceans that migrate there, have been protected by law since 1933.

51

The other shore of the Sea of Cortés is overlooked by the breath-taking landscapes of the big Sonorense Desert, which contains the El Pinacate y Gran Desierto de Altar Biosphere Reserve (Sonora). Here, the characteristic vegetation *Arborea xerofita*, composed mainly of *palo verde* (*Cercidium*), *huamuchil* (*Pithecolobinum*), cacti, and shrubs, grows on extremely beautiful and impressive volcanic formations, including craters, lava flows, and ash cones. In this region, summer temperatures can reach 120°F, whereas in winter freezing temperatures are common at night. Proceeding east, one climbs the Sierra Madre Occidental, whose spectacular landscapes culminate in the Barranca del Cobre National Park (Chihuahua). This mountainous area, which remains the territory of the Tarahumara Indians, is cut through by at least 20 canyons cut and is traversed by the famous Los Mochis-Chihuahua railway. The line boasts 39 bridges and 86 tunnels along a 406-mile route through canyons, cliffs, and pine forests, whose existence is guaranteed by the relatively humid climate of the Sierra. Once past the Sierra Madre Occidental, the visitor enters the Chihuahuense Desert (Chihuahua and Coahuila), one of the most arid and severe on the planet, where impressive calcareous mountain chains alternate with vast basins of plains in a land-

53 top left and right
Seemingly void of life,
the territory
surrounding the town
of Samalayuca, in
northern Chihuahua,
is actually very
important for its
natural heritage. Its
plant species, such as
the squat Ferocactus
wislizeni and the
prickly yucca visible
on the right,
constitute the "hidden
treasures" of this
barren region.

scape dominated by agaves and aloe plants (among which stands out the *Agave lechuguilla*), *mezquites* (*Prosopis juliflora*), yucca (*Yucca sp.*), and prickly pear (*Opuntia sp.*). The desert landscape is interrupted by wide depressions such as the Bolsón de Mapimí and the Cuatro Ciénegas (Coahuila), where a series of crystalline karstic-origin ponds constitutes one of the natural treasures of northern Mexico.

The Chihuahuense Desert, which extends as far north as the Mexican-American border – marked by the course of the Rio Grande (or Río Bravo, as the Mexicans prefer to call it) – is bounded to the east by the high peaks of the Sierra Madre Oriental. This chain is the southern extension of the Texas Rocky Mountains and is where the El Cielo Biosphere Reserve is located. Here it is possible to observe a curious mingling of desert, temperate, and tropical ecosystems. Continuing east, the visitor descends toward the lowlands of the Tamaulipas and the Atlantic Coast.

54-55 The pleasant territory surrounding Lake Pátzcuaro and the lake itself have made the region prosperous, furnishing abundant timber, fish, and several vegetable species, often cultivated on terraces, which have kept the soil in excellent condition.

54 top Fishermen are hard at work on Lake Pátzcuaro, in Michoacán, with their large traditional "butterfly-nets." On these shores, the Chichimeco people settled around A.D. 1200, subjugating the autochthonous population.

South of the Tropic of Cancer, the convergence of the two great chains of the Sierra Madre forms the so-called Central Plateau, vast highlands of volcanic origin that constitute and have always constituted the true economic and cultural heart of the country. The plateau is distinguished by an abundance of lake-filled basins that fostered the development of some of the most complex Mesoamerican civilizations, in particular Lake Chapala, Lake Pátzcuaro, and, above all, the Mexican Basin. The northern central region of the plateau, renowned for its mineral wealth, corresponds with the present-day states of Zacatecas, San Luis Potosí, Aguas Calientes, Guanajuato, and Querétaro. A large part of the northern area of this region is occupied by vast mountain and desert zones, whereas the area of Guanajuato and Querétaro, known as El Bajío, is characterized by a more humid and pleasant climate, as is the northern central part of the plateau. The latter region corresponds to the west with the coastal states of Nayarit, Jalisco, Colima, and Michoacán (whose Pacific coastlines will be described further on). Although they are mountainous regions, the climate is hot and humid (the famous blue agave from which tequila is made grows here), and at lower altitudes the higher humidity makes it possible for a tropical-like, lush vegetation to thrive. South of the city of Guadalajara (Jalisco), Lake Chapala is the biggest in Mexico. Surrounded by pleasant countryside, it is, unfortunately, highly polluted.

The most beautiful region in the northern central area of the plateau is certainly that of Michoacán. Dotted with volcanic formations, its heart is the gorgeous Lake Pátzcuaro, around which flourished the Tarasco civilization, the ancestors of the present-day Purépecha. In terms of nature, one of the most spectacular places in all of Mexico is the Santuario de Mariposas El Rosario (El Rosario Butterfly Sanctuary), in the far eastern section of Michoacán. Here, between the end of October and the beginning of November, millions of bright orange butterflies arrive from the United States and Canada, staying on until March when they migrate back.

The beating heart of the Central Plateau and of all of Mexico is the Mexican Basin, the ancient Anahuac of the Aztecs, surrounded by volcanoes and once occupied by the vast lake system of Texcoco, today almost entirely overtaken by the country's gigantic capital. The landscape of the basin alternates between snowbound peaks, narrow rocky gorges, vast cultivated plains, and remnants of the ancient lakes. A hint of what the landscape must have looked like in antiquity can still be found in the area of Xochimilco, where "floating gardens" full of flowers are bordered by rows of willows. In ancient times, the Central Plateau, with the exception of its drier eastern side, was covered by pine, oak, and juniper forests, today almost completely destroyed by man and replaced by semi-desert types of vegetation, prevalently cacti, acacias, and the characteristic *pirul* (*Schinus molle*), introduced from Peru around 1550. The existence of the lakes makes it possible to for abundant quantities of fish, reptiles, amphibians, aquatic birds, and insects to flourish, whereas in the past, rabbits and deer thrived in the area of the basins.

East of the Mexican Basin, the mountain countryside in the states of Puebla and Tlaxcala extends along the natural guideline leading from central Mexico to the Gulf Coast. This area is characterized by greater dryness, constituting a continuous strip of arid lands that rise from the Tehuacán (Oaxaca) region into the eastern part of the state of Puebla as far as the Mezquital (Hidalgo) region.

The southern edge of the Central Plateau is formed by the so-called Neovolcanic Cordillera, a chain of tall, perennially snow-covered volcanoes – each of which is protected within a national park – that runs west to east. They include the Nevado de Colima (Colima), the Nevado de Toluca (state of Mexico), the "couple" Iztaccíhuatl-Popocatépetl (between the state of Mexico and Veracruz), and Pico de Orizaba (Veracruz).

The Sierra Madre del Sur, with a variety of peak names and stretching across Guerrero, Oaxaca, and Chiapas, constitutes, from an environmental and climatic point of view, a sort of continuation of the Central Plateau, characterized by dry, striking mountain landscapes dotted by the famous candelabra cacti known as *órganos*.

At Oaxaca, the Sierra Madre del Sur meets the Sierra Madre de Oaxaca, giving rise to some of the most spectacular tracts of mountains in the country, featuring coniferous woods alternating with outright desert regions. The deserts give way to lush, tropical-like green areas running alongside low-altitude waterways.

In this region, where the temperate and tropical climatic regions meet, the biodiversity of animal and vegetable species has evolved to be one of the highest in Mexico. Besides its splendid cultural heritage, both archeological and colonial, the Sierra de Oaxaca holds surprises such as Hierve el Agua, where mineral springs have produced spectacular calcite "waterfalls" and icy ponds. The western part of the state is called Mixteca (in turn divided into Lower, Upper, and Coastal) and forms the territory of the Mixtecs, whereas the central valleys (Tlacolutla, Etla, and Zimatlán) constitute the heart of the Zapotec territory.

At the point were the three valleys come together stands the city of Oaxaca, capital of the state, as well as ancient Monte Albán.

58 Incredibly blue waters have earned these gorgeous rapids in the state of Chiapas, a bit south of Palenque, the name of Agua Azul. The roughly 500 waterfalls scattered across the area have the prettiest color in spring, before the hard summer rains.

59 top A few miles south of Palenque, the Misol-Ha waterfall offers immensely beautiful views of the lush vegetation of Chiapas.

59 center Though it is possible to swim in certain places, in general the rapids of Agua Azul are extremely turbulent. Two rivers, the Yaxha and the Shumulha, form this marvel of nature.

59 bottom The luxuriant lands of Chiapas stretch as far as the eye can see in the deep south of Mexico, at the base of the Yucatán Peninsula. The climate, equatorial in the lower region, varies to tropical at higher altitudes.

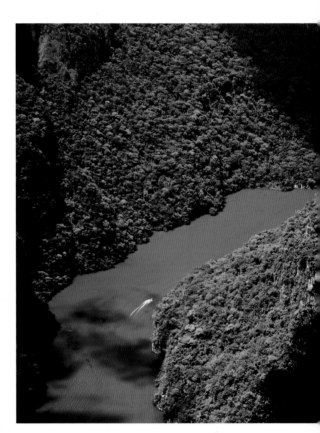

Once past the Tehuantepec Isthmus, where the two oceans are separated by no more than 125 miles, the series of mountain chains form a fork located in the state of Chiapas. The Sierra Madre proper runs parallel to the Pacific Coast until culminating at the Guatemalan border in the peak of Tajumulco (13,846 feet). The so-called Altos de Chiapas – with elevations varying from six to ten thousand feet and largely clad with coniferous woods – cross the central part of the state and then continue as far as Guatemalan territory, where the lovely Montebello Lakes dot the borderlands.

Between the Sierra Madre del Sur and the Altos de Chiapas opens a vast central depression, the valley of the Grijalva River, born in the Cuchumatanes Mountains in Guatemala and running across the state of Chiapas until it turns north and proceeds on its journey toward the Gulf of Mexico.

At the easternmost point on its course, the Grijalva winds into the spectacular Sumidero Canyon, where alligators placidly float between tall calcareous walls up to 3,000 or more feet high. Today, the Grijalva intermittently flows through large artificial basins created to generate hydroelectric energy for a substantial part of the Mexican Republic. Into one of these (Malpaso Lake) flows the Río La Venta, the waterway of another of the splendid Chiapanec canyons. This canyon cuts through the Selva El Ocote Nature Reserve, whose fantastic natural and archeological features have long been the subjects of much research.

62-63 *Acapulco extends along a magnificent bay in the state of Guerrero on the Pacific Ocean, due south of Mexico City. Behind the hotels, a chain of hills forms a rock bastion protecting this locality of legendary fame.*

The Pacific Coast, from the state of Sinaloa to the southernmost tip of Chiapas, is made up of a long strip of tropical terrain distinguished by thick vegetation, with an abundance of trees such as mahogany, cieba, and Spanish cedar. The coast also has important resorts such as Mazatlán (Sinaloa), San Blas (Nayarit), Puerto Vallarta (Jalisco), Acapulco (Guerrero), and Puerto Escondido and Puerto Angel (Oaxaca). From the southernmost part of Oaxaca and in all of Chiapas, the coast is known for its vast network of lagoons and coastal canals bordered by dense mangrove swamps. The wealth of these lake resources, combined with intense rains and the fertile coastal soil, made the Pacific Coast of Chiapas, known as Soconusco and famous for its cocoa plantations, one of the richest regions in all of ancient Mexico. This region was setting for the development of some of the oldest and most successful Mesoamerican farming societies.

62 top left The waves of the Pacific create long frothy trails along the Michoacán coast, between the beach towns of La Mira and Tecomán. This coastline, with but a few sparse settlements, is still rather wild.

62 top right Puerto Escondido, in the state of Oaxaca, only developed as a tourist resort during the 1960s. What is today a city, in 1928 was founded as a harbor for loading coffee exports.

63 left A fearless diver throws himself into the void off the famous cliffs of Acapulco. Timing is everything: taking advantage of the rising waters caused by a wave, the dive concludes happily.

63 right Puerto Vallarta, another big name among the elite famous beach towns, stands in the middle of the 60 miles of coastline of Banderas Bay, in the far north of the state of Jalisco on the Pacific Ocean.

The Atlantic Coast from Veracruz to the southernmost point on the Gulf of Mexico (Tabasco) represents the greatest stretch of the so-called *tierra caliente*, full of forest, agricultural, mineral, and oil reserves. The coastal strip, above all its southern part, is sprinkled with lagoons and is crossed by numerous waterways that empty into the Atlantic, such as the Papaloapan, the Coatzacoalcos, and the Grijalva-Usumacinta. The delta of this last-named river network dumps over 26 trillion gallons of wa-

ter into the ocean a year. The tropical vegetation of the coast stretches endlessly within the vast forest covering the northern part of Chiapas and the southern Yucatán Peninsula, which then continues on to cover a large part of northern Guatemala under the name of the Petén Forest. All of this region, which was the homeland of the classical Mayan civilizations, is protected within an international reserve formed by combining the Calakmul Biosphere Reserve in

Mexico, the Petén Maya Biosphere Reserve in Guatemala, and the Río Bravo Conservation Area in Belize. Noteworthy among the countless plant species living in the reserve are the caoba or mahogany tree (*Swietenia sp.*), the chicozapote or sapodilla tree (*Achras zapota*), the guayabo or nargusta tree (*Terminalia amazonia*), the ramon tree (*Brosimium alicastrum*), and the ceiba tree (*Ceiba pentandra*). In fact, some acres of primary tropical forest contain more tree species than the entire continent of Europe.

The extensive tracts of tropical forest are often interrupted by savanna areas characterized by low trees and shrubs, many of which (known as *acahuales*) are the product of thousands of years of human farming activities. The animal life of the forest is as diverse as its plant life: jaguars, pumas, ocelots, monkeys, snakes, deer, tapirs, and peccaries stand out among the thousands of species present, many of which are birds and above all insects.

66 top Lush palm groves line the wide inlet of Playa del Carmen, on the east coast of the Yucatán Peninsula in Quintana Roo. Today a full-swing vacation spot, in Mayan times this tract of coastline had a port.

66 center and bottom The warm tropical waters of Mexico's Caribbean coast are loaded with life and are therefore a destination favored by scuba divers. Caribbean reef sharks (Carcharhinus perezi) are regular visitors of the coast.

with white beaches and coral reefs, constituting one of the main tourist attractions in the country. From Cancún to Tulum, a line of vacation spots stretches almost without interruption, including popular locations such as Playa del Carmen, Xcaret, Akumal, Xcacel, and Xel-Ha, to which can be added the island of Cozumel surrounded by Palancar Reef, one of the most famous coral reefs in the world. South of Tulum, the Sian Ka'an Biosphere Reserve may be one of the most beautiful in Mexico. Here – in over 2,000 square miles of territory that UNESCO has declared to be part of the heritage of humanity, far from the crowded vacation spots to the north – it is possible to enjoy the combination of tropical vegetation with the Caribbean coastline. In addition, visitors can see animal life that includes ocelots, pumas, jaguars, howler monkeys and caimans, vultures, and eagles. Among the better-known representatives of the region's marine life are tortoises that deposit their eggs along the Yucatán beaches. The extraordinary variety of ecosystems within Mexican territory, whose conservation represents a challenge that must be unfailingly confronted, was in the past one of the main reasons for the development of complex and stratified indigenous societies, facilitated by dense trade networks that circulated the products of the various regions. The masterpieces of the ancient pre-Hispanic civilizations and those of the conquerors who came to pillage the riches of this splendid land today constitute a cultural heritage that blends perfectly with the country's extraordinary natural and wildlife settings.

Continuing northeast however, the forest gives way to tropical savanna in the northern part of the Yucatán Peninsula, today divided among the Mexican states of Campeche, Yucatán, Quintana Roo, and the independent nation of Belize. A vast calcareous plate forms the area where an intense karst phenomenon has produced a high number of caves and *cenotes* (wells). The eastern coast of the Yucatán Peninsula overlooks the Caribbean Sea and is lined

66-67 Cancún, along the coast of Quintana Roo, is lapped by crystal-clear waters, which offer extraordinary visibility, up to 150 feet. The fame of this place, however, is also due to its sand, bright white and super fine.

67 top Immersed in a luxuriant environment, the natural marvels of the Xel Ha National Park create an immense natural aquarium, featuring both salt and fresh water, just a few miles north of Tulum, on the east coast of the Yucatán.

THE ARCHAEOLOGICAL SITES

69 top left The Quemada, in the state of Zacatecas, was the main sanctuary of the Chalchihuites civilization, characterized by their integration with the nomads of the north. Large columned halls like the one seen here, connected with the meetings of warriors, were one of the main architectural contributions of the Chalchihuites society to the successive Mesoamerican culture.

69 top right Temple B of Tula dominates the central square of the Toltec imperial capital. On the top of the pyramid dedicated to Tlahuizcalpantecuhtli (Venus manifested as the Morning Star), Atlases and other sculptural pillars stand tall. The practice of holy war was associated with the movements of the Morning Star, the purpose of which was to capture prisoners for sacrifice.

68 Tzintzuntzan, in the state of Michoacán, was the most important capital of the Tarasco kingdom, a dangerous rival of the Aztec Empire. Among the characteristic elements of Tarasco architecture, there are the stepped circular podiums as seen here, known as yacatas.

68-69 The four Atlases supporting the roof of the temple of Tula are accompanied by pillars decorated with bas-reliefs of warriors and columns in the form of feathered serpents.

T he collection of archaeological treasures in Mexico is extraordinarily rich, boasting over 160 sites open to the public. A long yet ideal visit to archaeological areas winds through the three main cultural zones of ancient Mexico, which despite being universes apart were linked in ancient times by trading and population migrations. The northwestern border separating Mexico from the United States divides an area that from a cultural point of view formed a single unit. Paquimé (Chihuahua), a vast mud-brick city in the Chihuahuense Desert, belonged to the Oasiamerican world, and from the 14th century enjoyed intense commercial relations based on the trade of shells, precious stones, copper, and tropical parrots with the Anasazi of Chaco Canyon, in what is now New Mexico, USA. South of Paquimé, it is necessary to travel over 600 miles through the desert and over the mountains of Aridamerica – totally lacking monumental sites because of the nomadic nature of its an-

cient inhabitants – in order to reach the northernmost of the Mesoamerican sites: La Quemada (Zacatecas). This city was the main religious center of Chalchihuites culture, where between A.D. 550 and 850, the Mesoamerican civilization enriched itself by incorporating Aridamerican cultural elements. It had a defensive and residential function, but its monumental center, featuring a pyramid and a playing field, attests to the important religious role played by the settlement, corroborated by the large Hall of the Columns where meetings between warriors involved in the practice of holy war were held. In the vicinity of the shores of Pátzcuaro Lake stands Tzintzuntzan (Michoacán), one of the three capitals of the powerful Tarasco confederation, which around A.D. 1450 was able to resist Aztec assaults. The city, which must have accommodated a population of more than 30,000 inhabitants, is distinguished by its five *yacatas*, temples with circular grand staircases dedicated to the sun god Curicaueri and his four brothers. Moving east, the visitor enters central Mexico and encounters one of its wonderful cities: Tula (Hidalgo), the capital of the Toltecs between A.D. 900 and 1200. It is dominated by the famous Temple of Tlahuizcalpantecuhtli (Venus manifested in the form of the Morning Star) on which rises the Atlantes, big pillars sculpted in the shape of warriors. The Toltec mystical warrior probably has its origin among the Chalchihuiteñi groups, as indicated by the resemblance between the colonnade of the Burned Palace in Tula and the Hall of the Columns in La Quemada.

Tula and other cities from the same era aspired to play the role of the "earthly replica" of the mythical city of Tollan. According to Mesoamerican tradition, Tollan was the sacred city *par excellence*, whose image was probably modeled after tales of the splendor of the most outstanding metropolis ever in the Americas: Teotihuacán (state of Mexico). In the far northeast of the Mexican Basin, the monumental city of Teotihuacán rises majestically along the axis of the Avenue of the Dead, featuring the massive pyramids of the Sun and the Moon, which seem to imitate the surrounding mountains. The two temples are believed to have been dedicated to earthly-aquatic divinities, as the presence of a cave sanctuary below the Pyramid of the Sun appears to demonstrate.

On the other hand, the Temple of the Feathered Serpent, adorned with beautiful multicolored sculptures, was dedicated to the celebrated patron divinity of citizens in government.

Besides its grand temples and administrative buildings, there were hundreds of quadrangular residential complexes in Teotihuacán placed along the lines of its urban grid. In these "walled blocks," groups linked by family and territorial bonds resided, dedicating themselves to specific artisan trades. The splendor achieved in Teotihuacán, which between the beginning of the Christian era and A.D. 650 was the main Mesoamerican monumental city, is clearly proven by the richness of the dozens of murals embellishing its buildings.

72 top left The central patio of the Palace of Quetzalpapalotl was rebuilt so as to exemplify the main characteristics of Teotihuacán architecture. The porticoes surrounding the patio support roofs with painted pediments surmounted by an element like "merlons" called almenas, which in this case are sculpted in the form of a symbol of the year.

72 top right The entrance stairway of the Palace of Quetzalpapalotl is flanked by jaguar-head sculptures, one of which can be seen in the background. In the complex iconography of the city's architecture and in its relations with the ancient political organization, many secrets of Teotihuacan's past are still hidden today.

72-73 The restored columns of the Palace of Quetzalpapalotl feature complex bas-reliefs with images of animals, probably symbols of powerful groups in the city. There are birds-of-prey, seen both frontally and in profile, framed by water symbols like volutes and long lines of eyes. In ancient times, these bas-reliefs were embellished by inlaid stones and multicolor paintings.

73 top The Feathered Serpent, from the Teotihuacán era on, became a sort of universal protector of Mesoamerican governors. Important feats relative to the creation of the sun, man, corn, and the calendar were attributed to Quetzalcoatl (the Feathered Serpent).

73 center The walls of the Patio of the Jaguars are covered with lovely paintings depicting jaguars with feathered head coverings playing big conch-horns. In the upper band, the god of rain/Venus alternates with illustrations of head coverings that may have functioned as symbols of political power.

73 bottom Heads of feathered serpents emerge from the Temple of the Feathered Serpent, whose walls are decorated with a sculptural cycle depicting the bodies of serpents surrounded by aquatic symbols and wearing alligator-shaped head coverings, symbology that may have expressed the city's political ideology.

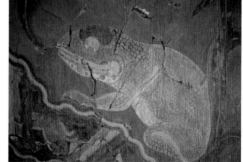

75 right The base of the Temple of the Feathered Serpents, in Xochicalco, is adorned with images of feathered serpents and seated governors, whereas on the upper part appear glyphs of tributary cities and cross-sectioned conch shells, symbols of divinity.

74 left Cacaxtla (Tlaxcala), the center of Olmec-Xicallanca power, flourished in the Epiclassic period (A.D. 650-900). The site has yielded extraordinary paintings of an overall cruel and bellicose nature accompanied by indecipherable glyphs.

74 right In the paintings of the Red Temple of Cacaxtla, designs associated with the cosmic circle of the gods of water can be seen, like in the case of this toad sitting on a decorative band containing fish, starfish, and other symbols.

74-75 The Two-Glyph Stela Plaza, dominated by the Grand Pyramid, is the main public area of Xochicalco, in Morelos, one of the cities that, after the fall of Teotihuacán, became the base of powerful political entities.

75 left The tzompantli was a ritual structure located next to the Templo Mayor of Tenochtitlán. From its base, decorated with images of skulls, rose a wooden rack on which were stuck the heads of sacrificed prisoners.

If visitors, when squeezed in by the imposing structures of Teotihuacán, find it difficult to imagine the ancient city's size, they will find it even more difficult to imagine the lavishness and splendor of Mexico-Tenochtitlán. The Aztec capital dumbfounded the *conquistadors* – only to be razed to the ground and then swallowed up by the colonial and modern cities. Only the ruins of the Templo Mayor remain of the ancient imperial capital, occupying a corner of the central square of Mexico City, between the National Palace and the cathedral. The temple, a double pyramid dedicated to Tlaloc and Huitzilopochtli, has been rediscovered thanks to a vast archaeological excavation project that has brought to light offerings of extraordinary richness, today displayed in the neighboring museum. Next to the temple, the rooms of the House of the Eagles with its colonnades and benches carved with scenes of warrior parades show how much the Toltec cultural inheritance influenced Aztec imperial ideology. Fortunately, in Mexico City, in the famous Square of Three Cultures, the remains of Templo Mayor and Mexico-Tlatelolco, the rival-twin city of Tenochtitlán, have been uncovered for all to see. Xochicalco (More-

los) was one of those settlements that were able to take advantage of the collapse of Teotihuacán around A.D. 650, becoming the focal point of a dynamic and warlike political entity that extended its control over the southern portion of the Central Plateau until A.D. 900. Dominating its monumental district (recently the site of a vast excavation project) is the Pyramid of the Feathered Serpent, featuring. bas-reliefs on its sides of the kings of Xochicalco seated among the coils of the divinity, accompanied by what can probably be interpreted as a list of cities that paid the capital tribute. Cacaxtla (Tlaxcala) also experienced its greatest period between A.D. 600 and 1000 when the Olmec-Xicalanca settled there, giving rise to a succession of lavish reigns. The walls of the buildings in Cacaxtla are decorated with some of the loveliest wall paintings in pre-Hispanic Mexico, in which the style of Teotihuacán has merged with technical and stylistic elements of southern origin, such as in the famous Battle Mural. On the hills overlooking Cacaxtla, the imposing ruins of Xochitécatl prove that for many centuries the valley of Tlaxcala had been culturally one of the richest and most dynamic regions of Mesoamerica.

76 top left A large field for ball games in an I-shape, or the pelota court, is also found at Monte Albán. The location of the structure, below the street level of the square, seems to allude to the role of the field itself as a symbolic point of access to the subterranean world.

76 top right The Hundido Patio opens onto Monte Albán's North Terrace, a part of the site that may correspond to a residential area for the elite. The fact that the most important noble families of Zapotec society lived here is attested to by the presence of several family tombs in the area of the terrace.

76-77 Monte Albán, in Oaxaca, founded around 500 B.C. by a confederation of different Zapotec groups, became the most important city in the Oaxaca Valley as well as the capital of the powerful Zapotec state that over the course of the Classic period came to dominate the entire valley and numerous surrounding territories.

77 top El Tajín, in Veracruz, was the most thriving city on the north coast of the Gulf of Mexico in the Epiclassic period. Its unmistakable architectural style is exemplified by the Pyramid of the Niches, whose sides are decorated by 365 recesses of obvious calendar symbology.

77 center For a long time, the construction of El Tajín was attributed to the Totonacs. Today, now that that hypothesis has been refuted, the ethnic identity of both the city's builders and many archaeological sites on the coast of the Gulf of Mexico remains one of the great "mysteries" of Mesoamerican archaeology.

77 bottom At times, ball games ended in the immolation of one or more players. In the bas-relief of the El Tajín field, a man about to be sacrificed can be seen (bottom). It is likely that games ending in sacrifice were not competitions but stagings with a foregone result.

After having crossed the extraordinary countryside of the Oaxaca Sierra, Monte Albán (Oaxaca) is reached, its monumental district situated defensively upon a hilltop. Majestic pyramid-shaped buildings encircle the large central square of the city, which was the capital of the Zapotec state for at least 1,500 years (500 B.C.-A.D. 1000).

Plaques painted with *danzantes*, portrayals of mutilated warriors, and stelae bearing the names of conquered cities in Building J indicate how much the element of war influenced the expansion of Monte Albán's power. The beneficiaries of this power were the noble family lines, whose city residences stood over splendid underground tombs with admirably frescoed walls.

Just as Monte Albán started to experience difficulties, El Tajín (Veracruz) was reaching the height of its splendor (7th to 12th centuries), imposing itself as the primary monumental center over the Gulf Coast. The structures at the site, framed by the lush tropical vegetation, are distinguished by the presence of niches and cornices that give the monumental buildings an odd "lightness." In addition to several pyramids (two of which are decorated by niches), some of the more noteworthy constructions include seventeen playing fields for the ritual ball game, one of the large Greek-cross-shaped enclosures called *xicalcoliuhqui*, and the residential buildings of Tajín Chico, among which stands out the Palace of the Columns, featuring scenes from the life of King 13 Rabbit.

Moving down the Gulf Coast, one passes into the original heart of Mesoamerica, in the land of the Olmecs, where sites such as San Lorenzo (Veracruz) and La Venta (Tabasco) are found. Among the large earthen platforms at the latter site (which was inhabited between 900-400 B.C.) an extraordinary collection of monumental sculptures was discovered. Today the collection is exhibited in the Villahermosa Museum Park (Tabasco), where it is also possible to see masterpieces of Olmec art such as colossal heads, thrones, stelae, basalt-columned tombs, and big mosaics in serpentine. Izapa, a monumental complex that flourished between 300 B.C. and the beginning of the Christian era along the Mexico-Guatemala border on the Pacific Coast, stands out among the sites of civilizations that inherited and modified the Olmec culture. The extremely plentiful sculptural *corpus* of the city, composed of more than 250 monuments, demonstrates that an elaboration of the Olmec iconography formed the base for the great classical artistic styles, among them that of the Maya.

80 top The palace built on the shores of the Otolum River was the dwelling of the royal family of Palenque. Its buildings are decorated with bas-reliefs in stone and stucco that recall their achievements: crownings, diplomatic encounters, wars, etc. The central tower was probably used as an astronomical observatory.

80-81 The monumental center of Palenque, in Chiapas, one of the richest and most important Mayan cities of the Late Classic period (A.D. 600-900), is dominated by the big Palace, the adjacent Temple of the Inscriptions, and the Temple of the Cross. The city enjoyed a strategic position on the border between the Mayan lowlands and the Gulf of Mexico.

81 top The Complex of the Crosses, in the foreground, was built by Chan Bahlum, son and successor of Pacal. Upon the death of his father, the sovereign undertook an ambitious architectural project intended to glorify his ascendance to the throne and legitimize his rule, during which Palenque reached its maximum splendor.

The classical Mayan world is today divided among southern Mexico, Guatemala, Belize, and Honduras. On Mexican territory such sites as Palenque, Yaxchilán, Bonampak, Toniná, and Calakmul represent this lost world that flourished between the 3rd and 4th centuries A.D. Palenque (Chiapas) may be the most famous of the Mayan cities, thanks to buildings its sovereigns Pacal and Chan Bahlum erected in the city center. These include the palace, the Group of the Crosses, and above all, the Temple of the Inscriptions, in which was discovered the sumptuous burial place of Pacal, interred in a monolithic sarcophagus whose cover was decorated by a famous bas-relief.

81 bottom On the roof of the Temple of the Sun, in the Group of the Crosses, remains of the stucco bas-reliefs can be seen that were one of the most typical artistic techniques of Palenque art. Even the tall "crest" that looks down on the building was covered by similar bas-reliefs, with scenes relating to Mayan mythology and politics.

*83 top left Pacal's
monolithic
sarcophagus was sealed
by a slab with a bas-
relief bearing the
portrait of the
sovereign who, dressed
as the Corn God,
returns from out of the
jaws of the Monster of
the Earth by climbing
along the trunk of the
cosmic tree. The
association of the king
with the divinity was
a typical characteristic
of Mayan political
ideology.*

*83 top right
The remarkable
structures of the
North Group are
some of the many
buildings that
compose the complex
urban fabric of the
city of Palenque.
Nonetheless, despite
two centuries of
archaeological
research, the
majority of the
ancient town still
rests hidden by the
vegetation of the
tropical forest.*

*82 top The Temple of
the Skull looks onto the
central square of
Palenque. The
excavations continue
to reveal new wonders:
under the thatch roof
visible in the photo,
the tomb of the Red
Queen was found,
a opulent grave that
may have belonged
to a lady in Pacal's
court.*

*82 bottom The Temple
of the Count in
Palenque owes its name
to the fact that Count
Waldeck, one of the
pioneers of the study of
Mayan cities, lived in
it for a certain period.
In fact, his fanciful
copies of the Palenque
bas-reliefs were at the
base of many false
myths surrounding the
Mayan civilization.*

*82-83 Pacal had
the Temple of the
Inscriptions built to
hold his own grave.
Although many
tombs of sovereigns
and nobles have been
found inside the
pyramids, the
primary function
of these buildings
was to act as a
podium for the
temples on top.*

84-85 The wall murals of Bonampak illustrate activities relating to the reign of Chan Muan II, sovereign of the city. Here, scenes from court, of ritual celebrations, and a splendid battle scene can be seen. These paintings constitute a fundamental source for reconstructing the clothing and costumes of the Mayan nobility of the Classic period.

85 top left Tonina, in Chiapas, was a powerful Classic kingdom dominated by the Dynasty of the Celestial Prisoners. The central monument stretches across the slopes of an artificially terraced hill, almost as if to reproduce a big sacred mountain. Many depictions of war prisoners stand out among the city's numerous works of art.

85 top right The architecture of Yaxchilán, in Chiapas, is distinguished by low, horizontal buildings topped by the remains of architectural "peaks." Yaxchilán was the most powerful city in the Usumacinta-River basin during the Late Classic period, and its governors came to influence the political life of nearby Bonampak and Piedras Negras.

84 top Though it was a Mayan town of secondary importance during the Classic period, the site of Bonampak, in Chiapas, is considered an archaeological gem because of the magnificent wall paintings it has yielded.

84 bottom The ruins of Yaxchilán, buried in the forest, are among the most fascinating of the Mayan world. From here came some splendid bas-reliefs, oddly sculpted along the lintels hanging over the entrances of the buildings.

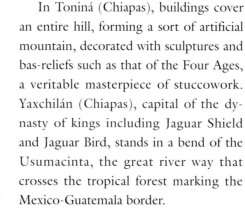

In Toniná (Chiapas), buildings cover an entire hill, forming a sort of artificial mountain, decorated with sculptures and bas-reliefs such as that of the Four Ages, a veritable masterpiece of stuccowork. Yaxchilán (Chiapas), capital of the dynasty of kings including Jaguar Shield and Jaguar Bird, stands in a bend of the Usumacinta, the great river way that crosses the tropical forest marking the Mexico-Guatemala border.

The bas-reliefs decorating the lintels and stelae in the city are among the best examples of the level of sophistication reached by Mayan sculptors. In nearby Bonampak (Chiapas), thanks to its "miraculous" state of preservation, it is possible to admire an example of Mayan painting in the Six Seas Temple, whose walls are frescoed with battle and religious ceremony scenes dating back to the reign of Harpy Sky II.

For many centuries, Calakmul (Campeche), a big settlement in the northernmost reaches of the Petén Forest, was one of the most powerful Mayan cities and the bitter rival of Tikal (Guatemala). In the imposing pyramid-shaped acropolis of the city, the tomb of Jaguar Claw, the most powerful sovereign of the Serpent Dynasty, was discovered.

87 top left The palace of Kabah must have been the seat of the city's reigning dynasty. In Puuc towns, the buildings, often a few floors high, took on a fundamental importance, becoming one of the most significant architectural elements of Yucatan artistic style.

87 top right The Palace of Sayil, in the Yucatán, may be the most beautiful building in Puuc architecture. Its three floors with columned entrances, united by one big central staircase, are decorated by mosaic designs such as masks of divinities and long lines of little ornamental columns.

86 top The five-floor palace in Edzna, in Campeche, dominates the main square of this settlement that played a fundamental role in Yucatán politics over the end of the Classic period and that constituted a kind of junction between the political entities of the south and the Mayan Puuc in the north of the Yucatan Peninsula.

86 bottom The arched doors were typical of the Mayan-Puuc style. The arch of Kabah was placed at the end of a sacbé, or "white road," the elevated roads that linked the various cities of the Yucatán.

86-87 Kabah, in the Yucatán, was one of the main Mayan-Puuc cities, which flourished at the end of the first millennium A.D.. The façade of the building known as Codz Pop is completely covered by mosaic masks portraying a long-nosed divinity, probably the rain god Chaac. Although hieroglyphic writing had widely declined in use with the collapse of the cities on the lowlands in the south, it was still being used in Puuc cities, as can be seen in the inscription in the foreground.

Going back up the Yucatán Peninsula, the sites of the many-columned Mayan styles of Río Bec (Campeche and Quintana Roo) and Chenes (Campeche) are encountered, which blossomed between A.D. 600 and 900 and are famous for their slender structures largely covered with sculptural mosaics. Proceeding north, visitors reach the sites of Puuc, a genuine link between the Classical Mayan civilization and the great Mayan sites of the Post-Classical period. Between A.D. 700 and 900, settlements like Uxmal, Kabah, Sayil, Labná, and Chichén Itzá thrived in the present-day state of Yucatán, developing one of the most sophisticated and complex architectural styles in the Mayan world, characterized by big mosaic masks adorning the façades of the buildings.

88-89 In the Yucatán, Uxmal, the most powerful Mayan-Puuc city, is dominated by the Pyramid of the Magician. The base of the construction has a strange shape with rounded corners, unique in the Mayan archaeological panorama. On top, a typical Puuc temple is adorned with geometric mosaics and masks of divinities.

88 top The so-called "Colombario" of Uxmal is actually made of the remains of imposing architectural crests. On these elements were placed sculptures and bas-reliefs that alluded to themes of religion and Mayan political ideology.

89 top The large masks on Puuc buildings have often been interpreted as representations of Chaac, the rain god. Another examination has, however, led to the conclusion that it represents several gods united by the "nose," in other words a protuberance on the face of a serpent.

89 center The long and low buildings making up the Nunnery Quadrangle of Uxmal are typically Puuc. The trellis motif decorating the upper part of the façade alluded to the royal mat, a sort of "throne" used by Mesoamerican sovereigns.

89 bottom The Nunnery Quadrangle, composed of four buildings around a central patio and thus named by the Spanish for its similarity to a cloister, was one of the most important complexes in Uxmal, probably used as lodging for members of the city's highest nobility.

90 top left The Red House is one of the buildings in Puuc style in Chichén Itzá, in the Yucatán. It has long been claimed that Puuc constructions were older than those of "Toltec" Chichen Itzá, but today it grows ever more apparent that the two artistic techniques co-existed for a long time, following the adoption of many stylistic elements from Central Mexico by the local Mayan population.

90 top right The Caracol, or "snail," of Chichén Itzá is a Puuc-style building dedicated to astronomical observation, an activity of extreme importance in the Mayan world. The windows that open in the circular structure are actually positioned to allow the observation of the sunset on days of the equinoxes and the summer solstices.

After A.D. 900, immediately following a period of rivalry with Uxmal, Chichén Itzá took on the role of the main political and religious center in the Yucatán, absorbing many cultural elements of Toltec origin visible in the Castillo, a pyramid dedicated to Kukulkan-Quetzalcoatl, or in the Temple of the Warriors, an authentic "copy" of Temple B in Tula.

Chichén Itzá, apparently built to be a new earthly Tollan, maintained enormous power until A.D. 1200, also because of its religious role.

In fact, the city contains a big *cenote*, a natural karstic well that was considered to be an entrance to the world of the underground aquatic divinities, an entrance into which countless offerings were thrown.

90-91 The Temple of the Warriors in Chichén Itzá is a sort of copy of Temple B in Tula. Also most likely dedicated to Venus manifested as the Morning Star, it was associated with the cult of holy war and the glorification of the warrior ranks, represented on bas-relief pilasters located on the top of the temple.

91 top The big columned spaces located in the area of the Temple of the Warriors were probably meant for large communal celebrations in which the orders of warriors took part, according to a custom developed within the Calchihuites culture and later transmitted by the Toltecs to the Mayans, who altered it.

91 bottom The entrance to the Temple of the Warriors is guarded by a chac mool, *a sculpture that originated in the sphere of the Chalchihuites culture of Zacatecas and Durango and that entered the Mayan world by way of the Toltec culture. In its lap, offerings and the hearts of sacrificed individuals were deposited.*

92-93 The Castillo, the big pyramid standing in the middle of the square of Chichén Itzá, was dedicated to Kukulkan, the Mayan version of Quetzalcoatl, the divinity adopted by the local peoples as a central element in a political and ideological model tied to the multiethnic nature of Post-Classic political entities.

92 top left The oldest buildings in Chichén Itzá, such as the House of the Nuns, the Annex, and the Church (in the photo), are clearly in Puuc style, as demonstrated by the fact that the important Yucatán settlement, founded at the end of the Classic period, began to develop as one of many Puuc sites on the Yucatán Peninsula.

92 top right Two snake heads emerge at the end of the steps leading to the Platform of the Eagles and Jaguars. The bas-reliefs adorning it with eagles and jaguars feeding on human hearts indicate that it was used for the sacrifice of prisoners captured by the two principal warrior ranks.

93 top The Upper Temple of the Jaguars dominates the ball court of Chichén Itzá, evidence of the connection between the ritual game and temple activities. The feathered serpents flanking the temple's main entrance can be noticed in the photo.

93 center The players on the field of Chichén Itzá, the biggest in Mesoamerica, must have been numerous. At the sides of the area, the teams are sculpted in relief as they converge upon the central scene featuring the sacrifice of a player.

93 bottom The presence of the large cenote probably dates back to the origins of Chichén Itzá's foundation. The cenote, a karstic well, was actually believed to be the place of access to the world of the aquatic gods.

94 top The main buildings of Tulum include the Temple of the Frescoes, with very beautiful and complex mural paintings, and the Castillo, the principal temple of the city, which dominates the site from atop its grand entrance stairway.

94 bottom It is probable that the ruins known as Tulum correspond to the ancient Zama, a trading center described by colonial sources.

94-95 Tulum, in Quintana Roo, was one of the main Mayan towns to rise along the Caribbean coast of the Yucatán Peninsula in the Late Post-Classic period. The location made it possible to control the maritime trade routes linking the Yucatán to the ports of Guatemala and Honduras. It was precisely one of their canoes sailing these routes to be encountered by Christopher Columbus.

When Chichén Itzá was abandoned around A.D. 1200, nearby Mayapán inherited its position, imitating its architecture in many buildings, the most outstanding example being the pyramid of El Castillo. However, around A.D. 1450 the hegemony of Mayapán also came to an end, when the Yucatán Mayan world fragmented into a series of small kingdoms, as magnificently exemplified by the ruins of Tulum, whose small buildings decorated with stucco sculptures and wall paintings overlook one of the most beautiful Caribbean beaches in Mexico.

96-97 On Paseo de la Reforma in Mexico City rises the Angel of the Independence, *a work by the Italian Enrico Alciati inaugurated by Profirio Diaz in 1910 to celebrate the 100th anniversary of Mexican independence. The urban landscape of Mexican cities is often distinguished by remarkable monuments, the fruit of the strong nationalistic spirit that has characterized the local upper class over past centuries.*

97 top left The Basilica of the Virgin Mary of Guadalupe stands on Tepeyac, the hill where the Aztec temple of Tonantzin, an earth goddess, stood, and where in 1531, according to legend, the Virgin Mary miraculously appeared to the Indian Juan Diego, canonized by John Paul II in 1992, on the 500th anniversary of the discovery of the Americas.

Mesoamerica was one of the few regions in the world in which an autonomous urban culture arose, in other words, one not derived from similar developments in nearby areas. When the Spanish arrived, Mesoamerica was peppered with cities like the Aztec capital Mexico-Tenochtitlán, whereas centuries before, even more impressive cities like Teotihuacán and Chichén Itzá had already risen and fallen.

Classical-period Mesoamerican urban culture, manifested in a series of monumental cities that functioned as centers of political, religious, and economic organization in the indigenous world, was characterized by a sort of bipolarity between two separate inclinations.

On one hand, with dynastic-type political entities – typical of the Mayan world but widely common throughout Mesoamerica – sophisticated monumental cities grew up, surrounded by gradually decreasing concentrations of living quarters, forming a sort of city "scattered" about the tropical forest, whose structure well reflected their inhabitants' family ties. In Teotihuacán, on the other hand, where settlement rules of a territorial nature prevailed, the model of the "cosmic city" developed, planned and more compactly laid out, neatly divided into regular city blocks. The inhabitants of these blocks probably had the same place of origin and in many cases shared the same trade specialization. In the Post-Classical period, this model was adopted on various levels by cities such as Tula and

Tenochtitlán, and even permeated into the Mayan world, giving rise to a "hybrid" urban format as found at Chichén Itzá and Mayapán.

The destruction of Tenochtitlán immediately following the Spanish assault of 1521 marked the final act in the history of Mesoamerican urbanism, at least from a monumental point of view. The sudden and violent defeat of the indigenous world led to the rapid introduction of the Spanish and European urban system, which quickly replaced the local one. As the indigenous cities disappeared one by one, the present-day Mexican territory filled with those colonial towns that still today constitute one of the main categories in the country's artistic heritage. Whereas the indigenous cities had largely been religious-royal cities, the colonial cities were rather administrative centers tied to the new economic system of New Spain. Following independence, the modern urban trends, such as the European-style ones of the *porfiriato* and the ultra-modernist ones of contemporary Mexico, were grafted onto this colonial foundation.

Whereas the coexistence of many different cities had always characterized indigenous urbanism, during the course of colonial domination, the process of hyper-centralization of urban functions initiated in Mexico City assumed such a pervasive role in the political, economic, and cultural administration of New Spain that the Mexican capital was transformed, overshadowing in some way the development of secondary urban centers.

97 top right
El Caballito is one of the best-known sculptures in Mexico City. The 1992 work "cites" another caballito, or little horse: in fact, it stands near the place where the equestrian statue of Charles IV was located, today in Calle Tacuba. Its continual relocation between 1803 and 1979 reflected the contradictory relationship between Mexico and its history.

98-99 Tijuana, in the Mexican state of Baja California, welcomes visitors from the United States with its more chaotic and "licentious" face, almost as if it were a Las Vegas of the south. The streets of the town are, in fact, dotted with the luminous signs of bars, nightclubs, and stores for bargain shopping.

99 top left The double soul of Mexico, divided between the glories of the past and dreams of modernization, is exemplified by this view of the Macro Plaza of Monterrey, in Nuevo León, dominated by the 18th-century cathedral and the Commerce Lighthouse, built in 1994 by the architect Luis Barragán to celebrate the centennial of the local Chamber of Commerce. From the top of the tower, a green laser beam lights up various points in the city at night.

99 top right The attempt to recreate the "true" Mexican spirit has led to the creation of structures such as the Pueblo Amico Shopping Center in Tijuana where colonial-style buildings contain shops and restaurants in which handicrafts and food constitute a sort of "business card" for Mexican-ness.

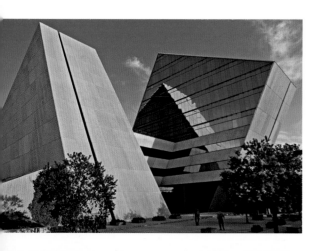

98 top The modern buildings of the Center of Advanced Technology accommodate the most important educational institution in Monterrey, the TEC, the most prestigious technological university in the country, where are large part of the youth destined to lead Mexico along the road to modernization are educated.

98 bottom The Tijuana Cultural Center is a sort of "window" to Mexico at just under a mile from the United States border. The complex encompasses a museum dedicated to Mexican culture and history, a giant-screen cinema featuring films about the nation's history, and, in addition to bookstores and exhibition spaces, a venue for cultural shows and events.

Despite the shadow cast by the great capital, the other Mexican cities did grow – often thanks to remarkable economic specialization – until becoming in many cases the present-day capitals of the now-federated states of the Mexican Republic. In these urban centers, just as in Mexico City, historical events have given rise to a stratified urban landscape, from which it is possible to understand much about Mexican history, from its remote pre-Hispanic origins to the troubled events of recent years.

An ideal itinerary for a trip to the Mexican cities must begin in Tijuana (Baja California), the ultimate border town, the true "gateway" to the country. Chaotic and disorderly, packed with nighttime establishments, rodeo arenas, cockfight pits and above all with shops crowded with thousands of Americans looking to take advantage of the exchange rate, Tijuana is a sort of fake image of Mexico that reveals all its contradictions and all its problems with the neighboring colossus of the United States.

Another side of the complex relationship between Mexico and the United States shows in Monterrey (Nuevo León), the third largest city in the country and the second-largest Mexican industrial hub. The city has always profited from its location near the Texas border, a factor that is excessively obvious in its modern architectural look, made up of skyscrapers alternating with colonial buildings among the modern parks of Macro Plaza, perhaps one of the most ambitious Mexican urban projects.

101 top left The cathedral of Guadalajara, built starting in the end of the sixteenth century, was not actually consecrated until 1618. One of the many earthquakes to hit the city made its two towers collapse (only one is visible in the photo), later reconstructed in its present-day form between 1851 and 1854. The new yellow spires have become a symbol of the city.

101 top right Real de Catorce, in the state of San Luis Potosí, was founded in 1778 following the discovery of silver mines. The collapse of the metal's price, however, declared its demise. Today partly repopulated, the city owes its fame also to the mountain overlooking it: sacred Wirkuta, where every autumn the indigenous Huicholes go in search of peyote.

100 top The Town Hall of Zacatecas has its headquarters in the residence that belonged to Don Vicente Saldivar y Mendoza, the son of the conquistador of the same name. In the middle of the palace, there is a lovely patio, typical of the colonial architecture of the period.

100-101 Declared part of the Cultural Heritage of Humanity in 1993, the historical center of Zacatecas contains buildings of great historical-artistic value. Among them stands out the cathedral, a splendid example of Churrigueresque-baroque style, built in a characteristic pink stone.

Just outside modern towns like Monterrey stretches the immense desert where some true treasures of colonial architecture recall the events of the conquest of the great north and its mineral riches. Cities like Zacatecas (Zacatecas) and small towns like Real de Catorce (San Luis Potosí) were born as important towns in the exploitation of the mineral resources.

The former, born as the "city of silver" in 1584, has continued to grow even in modern times, successfully preserving some of the more splendid colonial buildings in the maze of little streets at the base of the Cerro de la Bufa. The latter town has become one of the most famous places in inland Mexico.

Entered through a fascinating tunnel dug out of the rock, it boasted 40,000 inhabitants until the beginning of the 20th century, but the depletion of its mines soon transformed it into a magical ghost town in ruins. In recent years, it has attracted many Europeans who have settled there, creating a colorful international community.

The double-faced Mexican urbanism is magnificently exemplified by Guadalajara (Jalisco), whose colonial center, dominated by its famous cathedral, is encircled by a modern city whose industrial development has made it the second-most economically important city in Mexico, based on the textile, mechanical, ceramic, and leather industries.

Its three universities have also made it an important cultural hub.

102 top left The bell-tower of the Church of San Francisco, built between 1540 and 1550 and a cathedral until 1922, dominates the Obregon de Quérétaro Park, in the state of the same name, founded in 1531.

102 center left The effigy of Juan Antonio de Urrutia y Arana occupies the middle of the Plaza de Armas in Queretaro (for some, the most beautiful in Latin America) thanks to his having contributed to the construction of the city's famous arched aqueduct.

102 bottom left At the end of a street in downtown San Miguel, the massive structure of the parish church stands tall, built in 1683 but largely remodeled in 1880 by Zefirino Gutiérrez, who transformed it into an odd neo-gothic building.

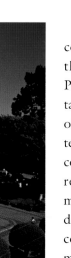

Proceeding toward the center of the country, the visitor encounters some of the most enchanting Mexican cities. Pátzcuaro (Michoacán), the ancient capital of the Tarascos, faces onto the shores of the lake of the same name, and its center is composed of a group of noteworthy colonial buildings. Originally the places of residence of the owners of the state's many mines, Guanajuato and San Miguel de Allende (Guanajuato) are veritable colonial treasures. They were made famous by the turbulent events of the Mexican War of Independence, many of whose main players came from the two towns. Although the fame and intensity of intellectual and artistic life in towns like San Miguel (now declared a national monument) have distorted their original character by attracting large numbers of tourists and foreign residents, Querétaro (Querétaro) remains an example of a colonial city that has maintained much of its antique appeal, easily noticeable in the little streets of its historic center.

102 top right
The ex-convent of San Agustin holds the Art Museum of Quérétaro, after having been used for almost 100 years as the Federal Hall. Its splendid baroque patio is a gem of the city's artistic heritage, declared in its entirety part of the Heritage of Humanity in 1996.

102-103
León Guanajuato, in the state of the same name, was founded in 1576 by Juan Batista de Orozco. Though it survived off of the mining industry in the past, today the city is known for selling handmade leather goods and, above all, its lovely colonial monuments.

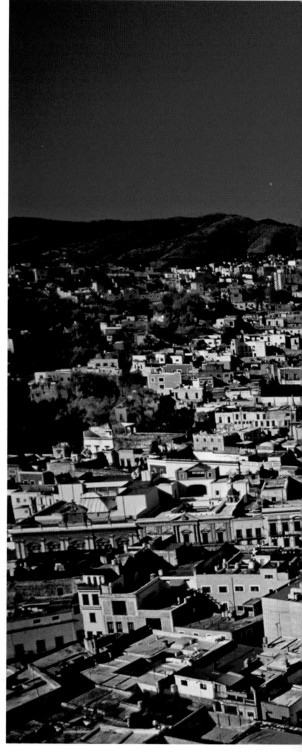

103 top left The historic center of Guanajuato features nooks and crannies full of atmosphere like the Square of the Baratillo, whose fountain was imported from Florence by the emperor Maximilian, a European Hapsburg.

103 top right The church in Guanajuato, also known as La Valenciana, features a magnificent baroque-style facade.

104-105 Plaza de la Constitucion, or Zocalo, is one of the biggest squares in the world, and it has constituted the heart of Mexico City since ancient times, when it was largely occupied by the sacred enclosure of Tenochtitlán. Today, the cathedral and the National Palace face onto the square: near the corner between the two buildings stand the remains of the Aztec Templo Mayor.

104 top left The massive structure of the Latin American Tower, 597 feet tall, has dominated the center of Mexico City since 1956. The Europeanizing tendencies typical of the Porfiriato are evident in the Palacio de Bellas Artes, in the foreground, the Bank of Mexico building, inspired by the Florentine Palazzo Strozzi, and the Post Office building, also Italianate.

104 top right The Capilla del Pocito, a baroque building whose dome is covered by azulejos, rose in the spot where the birth of a spring supposedly indicated the exact place where the Virgin Mary of Guadalupe appeared. The monument visible in the foreground portrays the apparition of the Virgin on the cloak of the farmer Juan Diego.

105 Luxury hotels, office buildings, and embassies line the Paseo de la Reforma, the Manhattan of Mexico City. Overpowering it all, however, is the Angel of the Independence, since become one of its symbols. At the base of the column, four sculptures represent Law, Justice, War, and Peace.

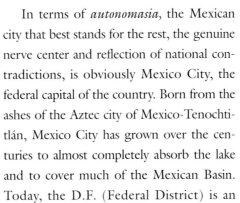

In terms of *autonomasia*, the Mexican city that best stands for the rest, the genuine nerve center and reflection of national contradictions, is obviously Mexico City, the federal capital of the country. Born from the ashes of the Aztec city of Mexico-Tenochtitlán, Mexico City has grown over the centuries to almost completely absorb the lake and to cover much of the Mexican Basin. Today, the D.F. (Federal District) is an

often decorated with vividly colorful murals, nature areas like the Chapultepec Woods or the floating gardens of Xochimilco, the impressive monumental heritage, modern and contemporary architecture, and above all, the city's intense intellectual life. This is fed by an incredible number of cinemas, theaters, cultural centers, exhibits, and extraordinary museums, among which stand out the National Museum of Anthropology, a

enormous and impressive gathering of colonial and modern buildings, wealthy residential quarters, and giant working-class suburbs where the number of residents probably nears 30,000,000 individuals. Known for the hood of smog enveloping it and its chaotic traffic, the city is too often avoided by tourists who miss the opportunity to discover its more attractive qualities. These include masterpieces of colonial architecture

veritable monument to Mexican nationalism and which holds one of the most extraordinary collections of ancient art in the world. Not all the city is excessively chaotic and unlivable: the neighborhoods of La Condesa and, in particular, Coyoacán, with pretty little squares full of cafés, bookstores, and handicraft shops, are ideal places for whomever wishes to get a taste of a different and enjoyable Mexico City.

106-107 A soccer stadium and a Plaza de Toros, true symbols of the composite cultural identity of present-day Mexico, stand out from the panorama of Mexico City. The practice of bullfighting was introduced by the Spanish colonists and enjoyed remarkable success: the Monumental, the biggest bullfight arena in the world stands in Mexico City.

106 top The University Library of the Universidad Nacional Autonoma de Mexico is one of the most representative buildings of the Mexican capital. Built in 1935, on three of its external walls the building features decorations completed in 1954 by Juan O'Gorman: enormous mosaics in multicolor stones summarize symbolically the history of Mexico, from the pre-Hispanic era to modern times.

107 top left The basilica of the Virgin Mary of Guadalupe constitutes the true religious heart of Mexico City, flocked to by thousands of pilgrims every year on December 12. In the area, several basilicas have been erected since the 16th century: the most modern, inaugurated in 1976, was designed by the famous architect Pedro Ramirez Vazquez.

107 center The resplendent, ultramodern building that holds the Stock Exchange of Mexico City rises on one side of Paseo de la Reforma, near the headquarters of important national and international corporations located in the area of the Pink Zone, one of the city's more elegant neighborhoods.

107 bottom The centuries-old Mexican "passion" for monumental art has made it possible for Mexico City to become a showcase of notable contemporary sculptural and architectural works, like the five "towers" erected in 1956 by the sculptor Matias Goeritz and the architect Luis Barragán in the Ciudad Satelite neighborhood.

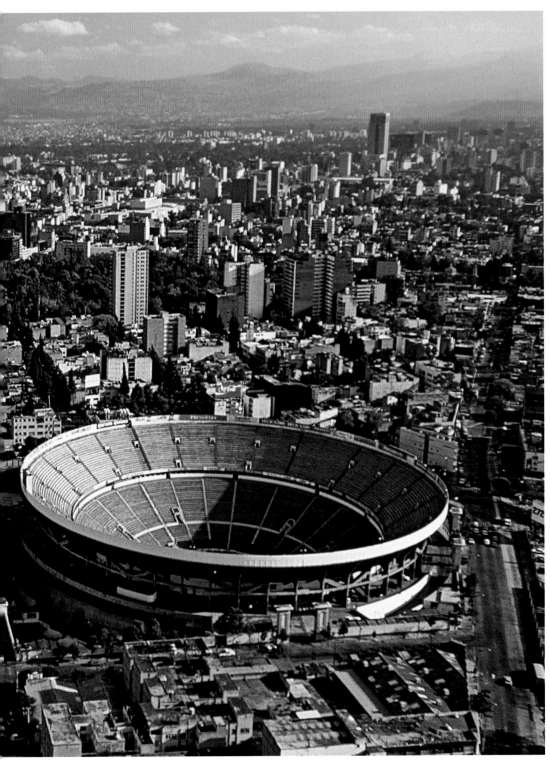

108 top and bottom The National Museum of Anthropology contains exceptional masterpieces of Mesoamerican art, in addition to pottery, textiles, farming tools, religious images, and traditional costumes.

Seen here are a stone that would have been placed in a pelota court, portraying a player in the act of throwing back the ball (top), and an eagle, which comes from the ruins of the Templo Mayor of Tenochtitlán.

109 left This bas-relief from Yaxchilán, displayed at the National Museum of Anthropology, portrays two dignitaries; the character visible on the right is busy handing the other a battle head covering.

109 top right The portico surrounding the patio of the National Palace is decorated with a famous mural cycle by Diego Rivera depicting several episodes from Mexican history, from its pre-Hispanic past to the Conquest, from Independence to the Revolution, and from the rise of Communist ideology.

109 bottom right The central patio of the National Museum of Anthropology is overlooked by the enormous "umbrella"-shaped central foundation. Inaugurated in 1964, the museum's new headquarters are the work of the architect Pedro Ramirez Vazquez and represent a summary of Mexican history told from a nationalist perspective.

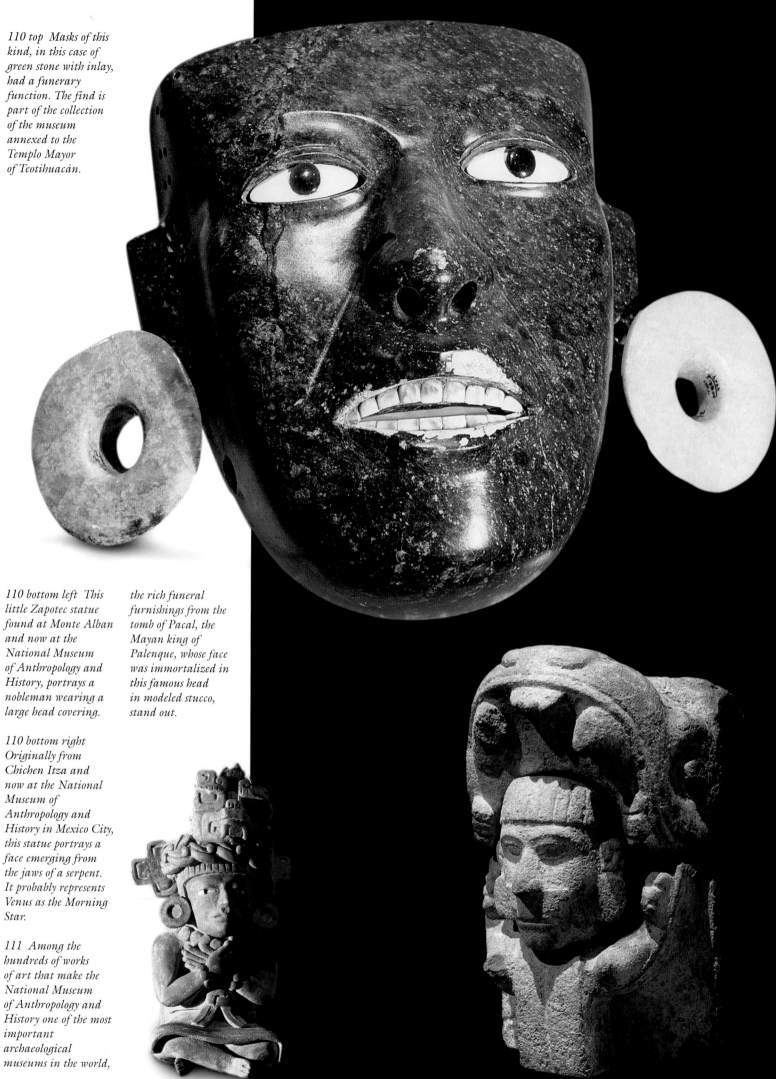

110 top Masks of this kind, in this case of green stone with inlay, had a funerary function. The find is part of the collection of the museum annexed to the Templo Mayor of Teotihuacán.

110 bottom left This little Zapotec statue found at Monte Alban and now at the National Museum of Anthropology and History, portrays a nobleman wearing a large head covering.

110 bottom right Originally from Chichen Itza and now at the National Museum of Anthropology and History in Mexico City, this statue portrays a face emerging from the jaws of a serpent. It probably represents Venus as the Morning Star.

111 Among the hundreds of works of art that make the National Museum of Anthropology and History one of the most important archaeological museums in the world,

the rich funeral furnishings from the tomb of Pacal, the Mayan king of Palenque, whose face was immortalized in this famous head in modeled stucco, stand out.

113 bottom left
and 113 top right
Tepoztlan, in the state
of Morelos, an lively
town populated
largely by Mexican
and foreign
intellectuals, stands
near Tepozteco, a

rocky peak on which
is found an Aztec
temple dedicated to
the god of pulque, an
alcoholic drink make
from agaves. The
town also holds
valuable examples of
colonial architecture.

112 and 113 bottom right The most famous colonial construction in Taxco is the parish church of Santa Prisca, built in the eighteenth century on the spot where the city's first church used to stand. The façade, begun in 1751, is embellished with precious architectural decorations in the Churrigueresque style typical of the period.

Despite the existence of these little "oases," in recent years many of the D.F.'s inhabitants have sought shelter in nearby towns like Cuernavaca (Morelos), the full-of-sights "city of flowers" that is quickly becoming a sort of golden residence for Mexicans and rich foreigners, including more than one Hollywood star, who thus follow a tradition begun by the Aztec emperors and perpetuated by Hernán Cortés and Maximilian von Habsburg. On the other hand, a bit more "alternative" or intellectual, little Tepoztlán (Morelos), a small town at the foot of the Tepozteco peak, has also become the hideout of a large international community.

Taxco (Morelos) is another of Mexico's small colonial towns that, thanks to its architectural heritage, has been declared a national monument. It was founded in the 16th century as a mining town for the exploitation of the silver resources, a material that has become the cornerstone of the town's identity. Even today, in the winding little streets of the historical center, over 300 silver shops are found, unquestionably an obligatory stop for visitors to the region.

114-115 From the patio of the church of Santo Domingo, the chapel of the Rosary can be seen, one of the jewels of Puebla's artistic heritage. The inside of the chapel, whose construction lasted 40 years (1650-1690), features intricate baroque décor entirely covered by gold leaf, which makes it one of the most outstanding works in Mexican baroque.

114 top The House of the Alfeñique (House of Nougat) was completed in the 18th century for Don Juan Ignacio Morelos and today holds a museum dedicated to the history and art of the state of Puebla. The building's strange name is owed to the fact that its pretty exterior decoration in brick, tile, and stucco recalls the sugar and almond candy produced in the city.

*115 top left
The church of San
Francisco was built
between 1570 and
1767 by the
Franciscans of
Puebla. The façade
is famous for the
tiled panels flanking
its majestic doorway
and for its tall,
four-sectioned
bell-tower. In the
building, the body
of San Sebastian de
Aparicio is preserved,
visited constantly
by people on
pilgrimages.*

The most Spanish of the Mexican cities, not to mention the parochial "adversary" of the Federal District, Puebla (Puebla) is often absent from the major tourist circuits. Founded in 1531 to overshadow the nearby indigenous religious center of Cholula, the city has over time maintained a strong Catholic and conservative personality, as reflected by its more than 70 churches and the thousands of colonial buildings in its center. Puebla is known for its hand-painted ceramic tiles (talavera) and for a few gastronomic specialties such as *mole poblano*, a sauce made of cocoa, hot peppers, almonds, tomatoes, anise seed, onion, garlic, and cinnamon that may be the most typical and well-known item in Mexican cuisine.

*115 top right The
ornate façade of a
Poblana church is
preceded by a pleasant
garden. It is said in
the city that the
churches are so many
so that you can visit
one each day of the
year.*

*115 center right The
cathedral of Puebla,
completed in 1648,
still has its bell towers
and decorated façade.*

*115 bottom right
Among the many
examples of colonial
architecture in
Tlaxcala, not
far from Puebla,
the church of San
José, whose
Churrigueresque
façade dominates
the city's central
square, stands out.*

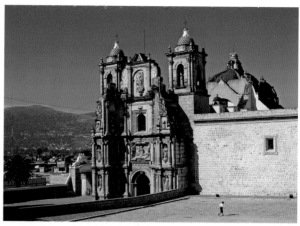

*116-117 and 117
center The cathedral of
Oaxaca, in the state of
the same name, was
built between 1535
and 1574 and was
remodeled several times
over the course of the
history of what remains
one of the prettiest cities
in Mexico, where the
colonial architecture
acts as a backdrop to
lively cultural and
tourist activity.*

*116 top left
In Tlacochahuaya,
just outside Oaxaca,
the church of San
Geronimo was built
in the 16th century.
The interior features
a cornucopia
of baroque
decorations, but
the church is famous
above all for the
French organ that
it holds, the true
pride of the city.*

*116 top right Facing
onto Plaza de la
Danza, the lovely
Basilica de la Soledad,
not far from the Zocalo
of Oaxaca, was
founded in 1692
in honor of the
patron saint of the
city, the Virgen de la
Soledad. Among the
hills visible in the
background, there
is the site of Monte
Albán.*

Oaxaca (Oaxaca), the most beautiful Mexican city in the opinion of those who write about it, is a true colonial pearl set in the valley of the same name that opens up in the middle of the imposing slopes of the Oaxaca Sierra. Its historical center features an air of times gone by, despite the remarkable development of this culturally rich and active city, recently accelerated by a new highway connection to the Federal District. Oaxaca is also the obligatory departure point for trips to the Oaxaca Sierra, the great Zapotec archaeological sites of Monte Albán and Mitla, or to descend toward the splendid beach towns on the Pacific Coast.

*117 top The
pedestrian street
known as Macedonia
Alcala joins the
square of the Zocalo
with the cathedral
of Oaxaca and
constitutes the main
shopping and tourist
street in the city,
dotted with
restaurants,
museums, and
handicraft and
jewelry shops.*

*117 bottom The tall
and narrow façade,
similar in layout to
that of the cathedral,
highlights the
monumental
appearance of the
church of Santo
Domingo, in Oaxaca.
The ex-Dominican
monastery annexed
to the church today
holds the Santo
Domingo Cultural
Center.*

118-119 An indigenous woman sits in front of the front door of her cobalt-blue and red house along Calle Matamoros, one of the main streets of downtown Oaxaca.

118 top left A child in Oaxaca carries a basket with a star-shaped floral composition on the Day of the Dead, which holds great importance in Mexico.

118 top right A group of Oaxacan women (the indigenous population of the city belongs largely to the Zapotec ethnicity) wear traditional clothing, an important identifying element that is worn with pride on special occasions.

119 top The markets of Oaxaca are meeting places for the natives, who gather to sell farm produce, foods, and handmade goods. Shopping or eating in one of these markets is a good way to get closer to the local lifestyle.

119 bottom The distinctive colors of the houses lining the town streets, further highlighted by the extraordinary light of the Oaxacan skies, give Oaxaca a characteristically lively and cheerful atmosphere.

120 top The cathedral of Veracruz, in the state of the same name, attests to the old wealth of what was once the most important port in colonial Mexico, founded on the spot where Hernán Cortés first landed. Still today, the harbor constitutes one of the city's main businesses.

120 center The fort of San Juan de Ulúa watches over the entrance to the port of Veracruz. Founded on the little island where one of the first Spanish expeditions to Mexico disembarked, the fort has grown over the centuries to defend the harbor from continuous attacks by pirates coveting the riches flowing through Veracruz to Spain.

Although Mexico's Atlantic Coast cannot be compared to its Pacific Coast, Veracruz (Veracruz) has always enjoyed a favorable position as the nation's primary port since the 16th century. Being a port city, Veracruz is a cosmopolitan city, with a significant population of people of African origin. Because of these characteristics, it appears to be a city with a very "Brazilian" atmosphere, merry and festive to excess; it is not for nothing that it is famous for its carnival, counted among the most important on the American continent.

The lovely fortress of San Juan de Ulúa, standing on a small island in front of the port (until 1760, the only one that was allowed to trade with Spain), is proof of the city's need for a defense against the recurrent raids of corsairs and pirates.

On the northernmost end of the Yucatán Peninsula stands Mérida (Yucatán), a small town with a colonial flavor. Built to counter the Mayan settlement of Ti'ho, Mérida was for centuries the headquarters of the wealthy agave fiber (henequen) plantation owners, but today enjoys a significant flow of tourists directed toward the Yucatán archaeological sites and the Caribbean beaches. Often in Moorish style, its colonial buildings feature the imposing cathedral and the House of the Montejos, the family of *conquistadors* that undertook the conquest of the Yucatán and that chose Mérida for their home.

120 bottom Three young women are ready to celebrate Carnival, the most important folkloristic festival in Veracruz, famous throughout the country. Begun in its present-day form in 1925, this holiday is the highest moment of celebration of the composite Veracruzan cultural identity, in which the black population, descendants of slaves brought by the Spanish, plays an important role.

121 Completed in 1598, the cathedral of Mérida, in the Yucatán, features a splendid example of the Moresque style of Spanish origin. Mérida was the principal colonial city in the Yucatán and is still today full of artistic treasures, characterized by a pleasant atmosphere far from that of the coastal vacation spots.

The small city that in recent years has become the true "face" of Mexico is certainly San Cristóbal de Las Casas (Chiapas), comfortably nestled in a wide valley between the wooded hills of the Altos de Chiapas. The city, characterized by its modest houses painted in vivid colors and embellished by lovely internal gardens, today seems suspended between the remote pre-Hispanic past and the globalization of the future. The native Mayans from the communities of San Juan Chamula and Zinacantán live side by side – even if not always in harmony – with the *coletos*, the mixed or white inhabitants of San Cristóbal, many of whom descend from the governing class of what was the main capital of colonial Chiapas. These local populations have mixed with the large numbers of foreigners that have in recent years poured into this beautiful yet paradoxical city.

123 center The pretty façade of the cathedral of San Cristóbal de las Casas in Chiapas is by now know as one of the more famous symbols of the lovely colonial town on the state's high plains. The church dates back to 1528 but was renovated often over the centuries: the façade, for example, dates back to the end of the 18th century.

123 bottom The Zocalo of San Cristóbal de las Casas is also known as Plaza 31 de Marzo. As can be found in the rest of this pretty city in Chiapas, the buildings surrounding the main square are quite low (except for the cathedral) and feature a somber elegance.

124 *Two little girls from Oaxaca de Juarez are dressed in their nicest clothes to celebrate the Virgen de Guadalupe. The indigenous population of the state of Oaxaca includes three ethnic groups, the largest of which are the Zapotecs.*

124-125 *Seeking shelter from the sun under their typical, colorful capes, women and children await transportation while sitting in a square in San Cristóbal de las Casas in Chiapas.*

*I*n many ways, Mexico is a country with a divided and fragmentary identity, which for decades has been asking itself how to form a united national culture reflecting the many ethnic and local personalities that characterize it. In fact, with over 60 native languages still spoken today, Mexico rates third in the world for internal linguistic variety, demonstrating the extent to which pre-Columbian Mexico's indigenous identity was not unitary. Rather, it was a true mosaic of languages and peoples only partially unified by a common economic base and, in some historical phases, by the activities of expansionist political entities like the Aztec Empire. Today the speakers of Mexico's 60 native languages – the direct heirs of the pre-Hispanic civilizations – number about 7,000,000, although over 25,000,000 individuals have at least partially indigenous origins.

The European peoples who arrived in massive numbers following the Spanish conquest represented only a final component added to an already complex variety; however, this component initiated an intense process of both ethnic and cultural hybridization. Although between the 16th and 19th centuries the Europeans and Creoles tried to reproduce on site a European-style society cleanly separated from the native one, this attempt did not prevent the formation of a vast layer of a mixed-race population as well as culturally hybrid traits. Primary among these were the profound Catholic beliefs tinged with traditional religious credence that were widely spread throughout the native communities.

After the Mexican Revolution, when the country found itself in search of a new identity that would mark a break with the past, the mixed-race identity was adopted as a national one that would transcend any single specific indigenous identity – often perceived as backward and reactionary – and launch Mexico toward modernity. Exemplary in this sense is the nationalist rhetoric expressed on the famous plaque standing in Tlatelolco Square commemorating the last bloody act of the Conquest, which reads, "On August 13, 1521, Tlatelolco, heroically defended by Cuauhtémoc, fell into the hands of Hernán Cortés. It was neither a triumph nor a defeat, but the painful birth of this *mestizo* country that is the Mexico of today." This same square, not arbitrarily known as the Square of the Three Cultures, is one of the symbols of Mexican cultural stratification. In fact, next to the remains of Templo Mayor from the ancient city of Tlatelolco stand the 16th-century church of Santo Domingo alongside the big buildings that are shining examples of modern Mexican architecture.

Mexico's entire intellectual life has long been dominated by the debate centered on the difficulties involved with merging the various traits of the country into a single national culture. A cultural political policy intended to integrate the native population into the modern and *mestizo* society was in place for many years. Recently, however, it started to become ever more evident that it was necessary to recognize the country's ethnic-linguistic diversities as a resource rather than an obstacle to progress.

125 top left An elderly woman in Huichol del Jalisco wears her traditional clothes, with the characteristic green blouse. These natives, who call themselves Wirrarika, safeguard many ancient traditions, including the ritual use of peyote.

125 top right With her baby safe in the typical cloth "cradle" that allows her to work and move around while keeping him with her, a young native woman scrutinizes the photographer in San Cristóbal de las Casas, in the state of Chiapas.

126-127 An lavishly attired indio dancer goes to the basilica of the Virgin Mary on the holiday of the Virgin Mary of Guadalupe. Mexican religiousness, still partly tied to pre-Hispanic traditions, is fully demonstrated on these radiant festive occasions.

126 top left On the eve of the Day of the Dead, two women place flowers and candles in a cemetery in Tzintzuntzan in the state of Michoácan. The cult of the dead has very deep roots in the cultures of the Mexican peoples, who used to associate creatures bearing feline features with the divinities of death.

126 top right Easter in a village in the state of Oaxaca: in Mexico, religious holidays can be grouped into three main blocks. Easter is included in the group of festivities that begin in winter, with Carnival, and conclude at the beginning of the summer, with Corpus Domini.

127 top The skull-shaped sweets, called calaveras de dulce or alfeñiques, are made with egg whites and sugar. Also of distant origin (skulls had great symbolic importance in Aztec and Mayan sanctuaries), today these objects are used as offerings to place on the altar.

127 bottom One of the more unique dances is that of the voladores, still going since before the Spanish Conquest. It is a sort of theatrical dance in which actors impersonate either the "monkeys" or the "angels." The pole shown here, about 65 feet tall, stands in Mitla in Oaxaca.

The mixture between native traditions and Hispanic inputs is visible in many aspects of *mestizo* religious life, like in the case of the pan-Mexican veneration of the Virgin Mary of Guadalupe, a genuine icon of the national culture in whose name immense pilgrimages are made to a basilica in north Mexico City that looks like a gymnasium.

Similarly, the colorful and strangely merry Day of the Dead, during which Mexico fills with decorated altars, piled with sweets and papier-mâché skeletons, recalls the festiveness and theatrics of the traditional native celebration.

In the northern lands, groups like the Tarahumara and the Huicholes are known for their still-surviving traditional folklore and, in the case of the Huicholes, for their important religious ceremonies tied to the use of peyote.

The most numerous native group in the country, the Nahua (1,700,000) is settled in the regions of Central Mexico. Descendents of the Aztecs and linguistically similar peoples, they often live in close contact with the Otomi (330,000). The Totonacs of the Gulf Coast in Veracruz and Puebla (260,000) still perform the *voladores* ceremony today, in which they spin around a pole until they fall to the ground, as prescribed by a tradition connected to pre-Hispanic solar cults.

In the state of Oaxaca, Zapotecs (500,000) and Mixtecs (500,000) are the direct descendants of some of the greatest civilizations of ancient Mexico, as are the many Mayan groups that populate southeast Mexico, such as the Chol of Chiapas and Tabasco (193,000) and the Yucatecas. Among the more culturally active Mayan groups, it is worth mentioning the Tzotzil (375,000), the Tzeltal (310,000), and the Tojolabal (40,000), settled mainly along the Altos de Chiapas in famous communities like San Juan Chamula, Zinacantán, Ocosingo, and Las Margaritas. Both the Mayans of the Altos and the Zoques of western Chiapas (34,000) are well known for the ceremonial complexity of the important celebrations held at the climax of Carnival, in which many elements of pre-Hispanic origin are evident. The church of San Juan Chamula is one of the more fascinating sights concerning indigenous religious practices, where the natives make offerings of obvious pre-Columbian origin inside a Catholic church, using bottles of Pepsi or Coca-Cola.

Although in most cases holidays of indigenous origin still celebrated today are either hard to access or by now have become so tourist-oriented that they have lost much of their appeal, an interesting atmosphere still revolves around some more common celebrations. These include weddings, sweet "fifteen" parties (a veritable initiation rite marking a girl's passage into womanhood), and rodeos. On these occasions, music and nonstop dancing, accompanied by rivers of beer and brandy, are a genuine expression of the deeper *mestizo* quality of being Mexican, which may find its most complete expression in the inevitable banquet. Whoever is lucky enough to be invited to a table laid with mole, pozol, atole, tamales, tacos, nopales, and to drink pulque, tequila, or mezcal will experience a most authentic encounter with Mexico.

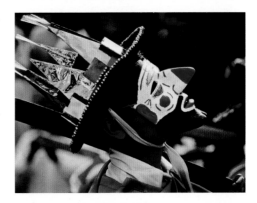

130 top A young Totonac woman from Cuetzalan in the state of Puebla wears her traditional clothes and a characteristic head covering made of different fabrics.

For the peoples of Mexico, the customary costume is more than a pretty outfit: it is actually a precious link between the lost glory of the pre-Hispanic era and today.

130 bottom A bird seller skillfully carries a stack of cages to San Cristóbal de las Casas in Chiapas. In Mexico, love of feathers and birds has distant origins.

130-131 Weaving techniques have remained unchanged for thousands of years. In the foreground, a Huaves woman from San Mateo del Mar, in Oaxaca, works on a telar de cintura attached to her hips.

131 top left A charro wearing a sombrero looks at the arena in which will be held the charreria, a well-loved traditional spectacle, which features horse-riding competitions and other displays of skill. At this sort of festival, a party with singing, dancing, and feasts, both men and women take part in special competitions.

131 center right A charro shows off his skill with the lasso. The origins of the charreria date back to the 16th century, when use of the horse, brought to America by the conquistadores, began to spread.

132-133 With a bandana and a Zapatista headband on his head, a baby sleeps in peace against his mother's back in San Andrés Larrainzar in Chiapas.

INDEX

136 *Figures of jaguars and warriors enliven the frieze on the* Temple of the Warriors at Chichen Itza in the state of Yucatan.

PHOTO CREDITS